PRAISE THE STORYTELLING BOOK

T0021447

"Anyone who has to write presentations or risks suffering death by PowerPoint has an opportunity to be saved. Today many of us spend so much time working with research and data that we forget to tell a structured and engaging story. This book takes the reader on an entertaining journey, using everyone from Charles Dickens to Father Ted to underline a better way of getting a message across. Everyone in research and insight needs to read this book."

PETER HAIGH
CEO, Mintel

"There isn't a dull page to this book. It fizzes with anecdotes and asides, which reveal the depths of the author's knowledge as well as the breadth of his experience. Anyone who can quote Bertrand Russell and Stephen Hawking on the one hand and Depeche Mode and Morrissey on the other is not someone stuck in an intellectual niche. There is a delight in language and some very good jokes. I, for one, would love to see tick-boxing become a competitive sport."

PATRICK COLLISTER
Head of Design, Google

"Anyone who has to write presentations or risks suffering death by PowerPoint has an opportunity to be saved. Today many of us spend so much time working with research and data that we forget to tell a structured and engaging story. This book takes the reader on an entertaining journey that solves that puzzle, using everyone from Charles Dickens to Father Ted to underline a better way of getting a message across. Everyone in research and insight needs to read this book."

PETER HAIGH

CEO, Mintel

"The Storytelling Book has the ability to dramatically change traditional presentations. With his understanding of the importance of behavioural economics, the art of storytelling and more than 30 years of experience, the author is able to combine valuable insights with practical guidance. This will fundamentally alter how we create presentations in the future."

PIETER J TWINE

General Manager, Loyalty and MySchool, Woolworth's SA

"Really readable, and makes excellent points. It has reminded me to keep the stories to hand when I'm writing or editing work, and not just the logical arguments."

SUE UNERMAN

Chief Strategy Officer, Mediacom

"We are all bombarded with multiple messages each day, so standing out from the crowd with a compelling story is becoming increasingly important. The Storytelling Book *is a highly readable and useful manual and provides both great tips on how to give meaning to your story so you cut above the noise and the easy traps to avoid when creating your story."*

ANNE BLACKIE

Head of Bids and Client Care, Grant Thornton UK

"In a world increasingly governed by metrics, data and analytics, Tas explains why the art of devising magical content has been tragically lost. Whilst we continue to wax lyrical about the need to enchant our audience, invariably what's happening is the essence of our creativity is being held hostage by the 'need' for ROI and what he calls the "arithmocracy". This book needs to be strategically placed on the desk of every business leader in the free world... before it's too late! Great, great book ..."

DEBORAH LEE

Social Media Branding Expert and
Forbes Top 50 Global Power Influencer

Published by
LID Publishing
An imprint of LID Business Media Ltd.
LABS House, 15-19 Bloomsbury Way,
London, WC1A 2TH, UK

info@lidpublishing.com
www.lidpublishing.com

A member of:

businesspublishersroundtable.com

Printed by Severn, Gloucester

ISBN: 978-1-911687-97-9
ISBN: 978-1-915951-06-9 (ebook)

Cover and page design: Caroline Li
Illustration: Laura Hawkins

THE STORYTELLING BOOK

FINDING YOUR GOLDEN THREAD FOR MORE EFFECTIVE PRESENTATIONS

ANTHONY TASGAL

MADRID | MEXICO CITY | LONDON
BUENOS AIRES | BOGOTA | SHANGHAI

FOR OTHER TITLES IN THE SERIES...

CONCISE ADVICE LAB

SMALL BOOKS: BIG IDEAS

CLEVER CONTENT, DYNAMIC IDEAS, PRACTICAL
SOLUTIONS AND ENGAGING VISUALS –
A CATALYST TO INSPIRE NEW WAYS OF THINKING
AND PROBLEM-SOLVING IN A COMPLEX WORLD

conciseadvicelab.com

CONTENTS

PART 3: TOP TIPS FOR STORYTELLING

TO EGG

INTRODUCTION

I started work at a long-dead agency, called SJIP, in 1981 (by which I mean it's long-dead now, it wasn't then; well, at least, not literally). I stopped full-time agency work in 1997, but have freelanced since then as well as being involved with ad hoc client and agency projects, training, lecturing and research.

I want to use a qualitative rule-of-thumb to calculate the number of presentations to which I've so far been exposed in my lifetime. I'm basing this on all the research debriefs (tracking, ad hoc and so on), client sales or briefing presentations in which I have been involved.

To those, I'll add the internal departmental or agency presentations and the "background information to get up to speed" decks for pitches or new projects plus the seminars and conferences I've attended, chaired or at which I've spoken. I'll also factor in the sales presentations where ads have been fanfared to 300 baying car dealers who still yearn for the days of the latest model being draped over the latest model.

Then, there are the away days, brainstorms and "workshops"

And that's without the presentations that I have perpetrated myself either single-handedly or as part of a brand team or agency pitch, or when the seventh new client of the year turns up and has to be inducted. Finally, there are those presentations relating to life outside, such as with my Phoenix Cinema hat, and even those that now seem an inevitable part of the education system (hello Key Stage 3 presentation from school).

On that basis, I calculate that I have been exposed to maybe three to five presentation decks a week. Taking a round figure of 200 a year, that makes me the "consumer" ("victim"?) of something in the region of **12,000 presentations** in my lifetime to date.

It shouldn't be difficult to understand that this is why I felt the deep-seated urge (please do not **under any circumstances** say "passion": already overused in our industry) to write this book: because, of all of those 6,000 decks and presentations, few have lingered.

The vast majority have simply been eroded by time's clearing-house. The relentless conveyor belt of memory has something to do with this, but surely, surely, more should have made an impression?

When and how did we reach this depth of banality and emotional sterility?

How did we become a community of deck-heads?

You may read this book in a number of ways. The straightforward linear sequential technique is an easy strategy to adopt. But I also hope some of you may prefer the DIDO route: if you wish to "dip in, dip out".

Note

The use of "we". Unless otherwise stated, when I say "we" I refer to the marketing, sales, branding and communications industries.

My pledges to readers:

I hereby pledge:

1. To try to nudge the centre of gravity in business closer to the end of the spectrum called storytelling (the home of writing, pleasure and rhetoric).

2. Not to use the word "paradigm", the "Sistine Chapel story" or any marketing clichés, or at least, not knowingly: look elsewhere if you seek expressions such as "pushing the envelope out of the box", "intense indulgence" or "elongating the click stream".

3. Not to "empower" anyone unless they specifically request this.

4. Not to include any Greek letter-bearing mathematical symbols or equations. If you are looking for $\sigma\sqrt{\tau}$, you have chosen to alight at the wrong station: if acclaimed theoretical physicist Stephen Hawking was happy to leave out all equations on the basis that he would halve his potential readership with each equation included, I am too.

5. Not to leave you bored and synaptically bludgeoned by the time you reach page 30. To paraphrase literary theorist Mary Louise Pratt: "How could such interesting people, doing such interesting things in such an interesting industry produce such dull books?"

6. To create a series of incidental (or uncidental) findings and ideas through the book, which you can cheerfully plagiarize (* legals permitting).

7. To try to create a compendium of obliquity, a serendipitous patchwork of ideas

Stories. We all know them, we all love them. So how can storytelling help us increase our chances of success in our presentations?

Sad, but true, we often forget that all of us in sales, marketing and communications are – at least partly – in the business of storytelling. We seem to have fallen headlong into a culture in which business thinking, business talking and business doing have been overtaken by a system that is contrary to our hard-wired storytelling instincts. This leads to ineffective communication and also makes us less happy human beings.

In the business world, we are confronted with a wall of homogenized indifference. In meetings, we are assaulted with PowerPoint (definition: "for people in power who can't make their point") or the triangles, arrows, graphs and bullet points that assume a strangely narcoleptic power.

When creating communications, we insist on cluster-bombing with messages, using steroidal media strategies from a bygone era. In pretty much every business sector, all the brands do the same research, ask the same questions of the same people and act surprised when the reaction from their target audience is homogenized apathy rather than meaningful differentiation. Sales forces routinely batter prospective customers into submission with an array of bytes, bullets and bluster.

In trying to remind ourselves of our instincts, we need to create something that leads to "differentiated talkability" rather than rely on an accumulated tradition of iterations, built on lazy post-rationalized truths and systems of behaviour and communications designed a century ago, in the Machine Age. The nightmare of imprecision, and the militant reductionism that has led to runaway measurement spitefully ignore our human emotions and diversity.

One of the key deficits is an unrelenting barrage of messaging with no attention paid to structure and editing. To remedy this, we need to find our "golden thread" which gives our communication a structure that will help our audience.

So: as in all great storytelling, as we shall see later, this is a three-act framework.

Part 1 will focus on the *why* of storytelling, taking aim at the system that has concealed our natural story-telling tendencies in favour of militaristic truth-telling and homogenized communication.

In **Part 2**, we will explore how to build a culture of communication, individually and collectively, that is more creative, more distinctive and more fulfilling.

Part 3 will concentrate on the *how* of storytelling, by showing how some of the techniques and approaches to storytelling can transform and transport your presentations.

HOW BUSINESS LOST THE ART OF STORYTELLING

A) THE LOVE AFFAIR WITH BAD SCIENCE

"What men seek is not knowledge, but certainty."

(Bertrand Russell, British philosopher)

INTRODUCTION: THE SCIENCE BIT

I want to explore *why* the art of storytelling has been lost in business –especially in how we present – and instead replaced with a mechanistic, reductive form of communication that has become so unhelpful and clichéd that it is nothing more than a meaningless and unfulfilling fog for those of us stuck on the inside.

In particular, I want to start by examining what has gone wrong in the business of communication and why the industry seems to have elevated efficiency and accountability so far ahead of creativity and imagination. But first, I need to "put up some scaffolding" for what comes later.

Let's start with what is known in the cosmetics and toiletries communications sector as the "science bit".

Anyone who frequents business conferences is subjected to an outpouring of dismal negativity that is reflected in the business media with increasing frequency. This includes marketeers bemoaning the failure rates of new products, or the glacial speed of getting new products to market; communications agencies lamenting that they are not producing (or being allowed to produce) cutting-edge ideas for their clients (who are, in turn, putting their best ideas to the sword of research); and creatives, usually at the sharp end, turning to (or turning on?) their planners to get them out of this "research and destroy" culture. Not to be outdone, agency planners then pass the buck to the market researchers, accusing them of bringing nothing new to creative development or brand measurement.

What lies beneath this malaise, I believe, is a stubborn and rearguard belief in a theory of business practice which is informed by "the science of management". This harks back to a bygone era and has never been fully unravelled or rolled back.

This theory is deeply flawed in two ways.

First, it is based on the wrong type of science: a worldview that is reductionist, mechanistic and based on "physics envy", the hope that everything – and everyone – can be reduced to pliable, predictable atoms.

It is fascinated with what I call "arithmocracy", a culture that is breeding and spreading across many domains beyond business, from our education system to the National Health Service in the UK, in which accountability has created a culture of obedience to the "god of numbers" and an order within society who put the "anal" in "analysis".

I would like to argue for a different culture to replace this tired and outmoded mechanistic model, one that is based on new thinking emerging within the sciences and has greater relevance to business, marketing and communication, with its emphasis on biology and the living organism that is inherently messy and complex but which can learn and adapt. This new model favours patterns and networks, rather than fixed essences, and is more interested in systems and their interactions than in the isolated performance of discrete parts.

The second radical flaw in the existing theory of business practice is that it gives too much weight to science itself at the expense of art or creativity. Though the methods of science are important for evaluation and measurement and the process towards ever-greater accountability has been a cornerstone of systems that extend far beyond that of business ROI, the spark that turns a product into a brand, or a message into a meme, draws its strength from the creative process.

At the heart of this problem is a reliance on, and envy of, the sanctity of science (or at least, one specific version of it): namely, physics.

B) WHY BUSINESS HAS PHYSICS ENVY

Since the publication in 1911 of The *Principles of Scientific Management*, written by American mechanical-engineer-turned-business-thinker Frederick Winslow Taylor, a certain type of system took hold in (mainly larger) US conglomerates and spread throughout the business world. An engineer by training, Taylor propagated the view of science as that of the clockwork, atomistic, push-me-pull-you, tick-tock-tick-tock, one-size-fits-all engine. Put this in here, and that comes out there.

Even forgetting that this was written at a time when relativity, quantum mechanics and the Copenhagen interpretation were on the verge of upsetting Newton's applecart, the tenets of this management worldview have remained as stubbornly persistent as the product claims made in the typical soap powder ad.

Based on Taylor's experience with pig-iron, he set in motion a theory of management that attempted to universalize its relevance from the machine shop into the broader domain of the human world. The theory assumed an almost messianic status, achieving remarkable academic credibility and even winning the approval of Russian communist leader, Lenin.

This was management of a factory, with people as cogs, reductionist efficiency as the dominant metaphor and a system that would guarantee the three cornerstones of a contented manager:

predictability, consistency and controllability. Taylorism begat Fordism (named after Henry Ford: "The average worker wants a job where he doesn't have to think") and from Fordism was constructed much of the management practice that was built in the US and then exported.

In this scheme, the manager is the omniscient and all-powerful scientist manipulating the passive worker. Scientific management saw its workers predominantly as "intelligent gorillas".

Many managers have been trained to operate with the scientific mindset in place (either explicitly or unwittingly). This has caused a conflict between the model of science they have, of order through analysis, predictability and certainty, and the operating system of the world in which their companies work, which is increasingly chaotic, unpredictable and uncertain.

But many of Taylor's so-called "sacred laws" were little more than post-rationalized conveniences, which could not sustain the definition of "science". Scientific management was instead more of a justification for an elitist managerial tyranny, where the counting was a method for oppressing the counted. As someone once said of reductionism: "it's a great method unless you're the one being reduced".

A new version of this attitude, "Digital Taylorism" may even be with us now according to Cardiff Professor of Social Sciences, Philip Brown. This new 21st century strain transfers the dehumanizing core of Taylor's mechanistic vision by translating the output of knowledge workers into codified practices and rules into software packages and templates that can be outsourced to cheaper (and often non-carbon-based) alternatives.

C) LIVING IN AN ARITHMOCRACY

"Everything counts [in large amounts]."

(Depeche Mode single from 1983)

I use the term "arithmocracy" to describe a system that I find increasingly pernicious and prevalent, and not just in the domain of business.

There are two variants to the definition:
a) The system of government whereby the pursuit of numerical solutions leads to runaway measurement at the expense of imagination, creativity and fulfilment.
b) A ruling class (as in democracy, autocracy), which derives its power not through intelligence or merit but by means of its access to and control of numbers.

The explosion in big data and data-generating potential over recent decades has brought undoubted benefits to areas as diverse as health (decoding the genome) as well as business.

According to a recent pronouncement by Mckinsey Global Institute, analysing large data sets is going to be central to transforming economies and delivering a new wave of productivity growth and consumer surplus.

The exponential explosion in social media and its metrics, multimedia communications and the "internet of things" (or pervasive computing) and the ubiquity of algorithms will make data-mining more demanding and more will be demanded of it.

But as with any technological advance, trailing behind it are implications that are not altogether clear.

Having had an active role in developing and evaluating marketing campaigns, it is hard to avoid reminiscing wistfully about the days when accountability had not become the universal idol of worship.

But, this is not exclusive to marketing. The veneration of arithmocracy has seeped through society almost without us realizing.

There are some siren voices declaiming that there is just too much counting in our society now, and speaking out against the deadening effect of statistics.

Yet, there has probably never been a time in history that measures as much as we do now. I want to examine whether this trend towards arithmocracy in society tells us anything about the context in which marketing is currently operating.

Behind the rhetoric here is a simple statement: that so often, what is really important can't be measured. What can be measured is measured, and as a result the flood of calculation directs us away from what really matters. But the boom in auditors, accountants, procurement departments and even (dare I say it) pollsters and researchers, has created a sort of self-perpetuating oligarchy of datacrats, fuelling a form of "runaway measurement".

THE SQUARE ROOT OF THE PROBLEM

In terms of our interest in numbers, it was inevitably the Greeks who started it all off, chiefly Pythagoras of Samos.

The Greeks had always been great followers of "mousike", literally anything governed by the muses. Indeed, they saw music as fundamental and timeless, just like the soul.

Pythagoras was a great thinker who defied categorization; he coined the word "philosophos" (lover of wisdom) and preached a gospel based on the inter-connectedness of all things. More particularly, he discovered the correspondence of the abstract world of music with the equally abstract domain of numbers. Pythagoras made explicit the link between the natural harmony in the universe, that comes from the beauty of number, the role of music and the divine cosmos (Greek for "order").

Behind this lies the danger that numbers count for more than words or ideas. In so many public contexts nowadays (take politics), something cannot be stated without recourse to some incontrovertible statistical nugget. One does not have to rely on that quote to feel that the reliance on numbers (as gods) has become excessive, and that sometimes we just have to learn to rely on words instead of the cosy comfort of a simple number, the lure of the single criterion.

But this obsession is not restricted to the world of brands and communication. Parents will realize that schools are now mired in a process of measurement and evaluation that is on the verge of overwhelming everything in its path. The search for the perfect proxy for "quality", not to mention the recent addition of more criteria, such as CVA [contextual value-added] based on other characteristics known to affect pupil achievement has left many parents, teachers and governors struggling to evaluate the "purchasing decision".

It is not immediately clear whether this system change has led to any *overall* improvement in standards.

Perhaps this system might seem to remind readers of one Thomas Gradgrind, from Charles Dickens's novel Hard Times. He was only too willing to expound his theory of education:

> *"Now what I want is facts. Teach these boys and girls nothing but facts. Plant nothing else and root out everything else."*

You'd think that Gradgrind would have appreciated the relentless intensity of testing that our children enjoy/endure. According to recent figures, the human cost of this system is that the average student in an English school has to take more than 100 formal tests between the age of 4 and 18. What is the financial cost of all this? About £250 million to run and administer all the exams.

The US is no different. President Barack Obama weighed in against test-driven outcomes, using a well-known saying that typifies much of what we are railing against in the wider environment.

> "There's a saying in Illinois I learned when I was down in a lot of rural communities. They said, 'Just weighing a pig doesn't fatten it.'"

As they say, it's easier to count the bottles than describe the wine.

Another way of putting it is to say that you won't get much meaning from a mean.

Another instance of this tendency to "doctor the figures", and one which arises in similar fashion from the political imperative for target-setting and accountability, is the UK health service, the NHS.

As with education, the move towards increasing accountability and measurement had led to various targets being imposed on the NHS, ostensibly to improve areas such as speed of service.

Such had been the pressure to meet targets that these health trusts resorted to some quite imaginative methods of getting people taken off the list. At one trust, staff wrote to patients and asked them when they were going on holiday. They then offered them surgery during these weeks – allowing the trust to suspend them from the list when the patient was forced to turn it down.

Or take the new targets for the police force. Performance measures such as response time and clear-up rates have now come to the foreground. But what has happened in this case is that the police now complain that too much of their time is occupied with administrative tasks at the expense of helping the public by actually catching criminals.

We are beginning to turn pupils into machines for passing exams, police into paper-pushers, and doctors into managers. Paper [often in the form of spreadsheets] is fast becoming the most prominent and valued output of many of our fundamental social institutions, and those who succeed most in this system are those who can best meet the needs of the paperwork.

D) MAKING PREDICTIONS

"It's Hard Making Predictions. Especially About The Future."

(Yogi Berra, American former Major League Baseball player/manager)

Financial expert and writer Nassim Nicholas Taleb's book *The Black Swan* became something of a business bible for the way in which it seemingly foretold the recent financial meltdown. But before that, in his previous book *Fooled By Randomness* the author had investigated similar territory: the extent to which we are so deluded in our belief that we did in fact predict what happened in the past that we believe we can do the same with the future. This is because we are hard-wired to ignore all evidence that we do not see and programmed to be blind to the possibility of randomness.

One of our many design faults is a failure to forecast, or deal with, the notion of unpredictability, and a general aversion to the non-linear, or the unknown (what Taleb labels Black Swan events).

Now, anyone who has spent time working within a culture that has a central atrium with a shrine devoted to "the five-year plan" has figured out in their heart-of-hearts that much of it is a concocted blend of wish-fulfilment, rationalization of job functions and existing systems of finance and corporate culture.

Yet once there is a plan, which in my experience has in all likelihood been based on "last year +3%", everything becomes a *fait acccompli* in pursuit of that plan; on the other hand, the world upon which that plan was based has almost certainly moved on, leaving the plan marooned on its own island of self-serving certainty.

It seems that we are just unable to accept the reality that human behaviour's natural unruliness is something that just cannot be explained and encompassed perfectly by theoretical models.

E) LET'S DE-MILITARIZE MARKETING

We cannot pass over the question of deleterious thinking in business without having a Quixotic tilt at the militarization of marketing and business in general (pun intended).

Whenever I am running workshops and I invite people to ponder how much of our everyday business language is based on the metaphor of warfare, I am surprised by how few examples emerge spontaneously. Usually we get "battle plans" or "guerrilla marketing", but the implicit (as so often with unsurfaced assumptions) goes unnoticed. So let's surface a few assumptions about the role of what Oliver Stone would almost certainly label the "military-marketing complex":

- *Strategy.* As a (still active) planner I am contractually obliged to use the word "strategy" at least once a paragraph (or a sentence if spoken. Sometimes this can make for a stilted social life).
  - Yet we too often take for granted its military origins. The word is derived from the Greek word for "general" [strategos] and therefore suggests a panoramic overview of decision-making and a sense of authoritarian control.
- Often contrasted with strategy is "tactics". From the word for "arrangement" (as in taxidermy, the "arrangement of skin") this is more about the disposition of forces under the instruction of the strategy, and is therefore more about spontaneous and short-term response.

- Perhaps the most implicitly unexamined is our old friend "target". From an old French word for "shield" this too has become freighted with a whole phalanx of meanings.
  - In business we "hit" the target, it is a passive vehicle or the butt (for example of a joke). "Ready! Aim! Fire!" Media schedules tend to take this metaphor to its limits, with talk of "impressions" and blitzes,even "bombing".
  - All of these layers are at best irrelevant to the current media environment where the talk is of creative collaboration, conversation, co-creation and "we-think".
- *Campaign:* again a word that most of those who work in marcomms or sales can probably not see through anymore for the fog of accretion. But take it out of its snug-fitting marketing jacket, and you can see underneath its proud battle-scars.
  - Campaigns were the activities of armies in the countryside or field (French "campagne" still means "countryside" from the Latin "campus" field; also still nestling beneath the famous avenue in Paris, the Champs Élysées – the Elysian Fields).
  - But it acts as a key rampart in the edifice of military marketing.
- *Bullets and bullet points.* Yes, it's time to rail against PowerPoint, or at least against a certain (mis-/ab-) use of it. Anyone who has had to endure a lengthy presentation, a conference or an "away day" only to be caught in a hail of bullet points knows the feeling of pain and agonizing sense of surrender that ensues.
- Then you can add a plethora of other military terms from the "battle for market share" or the "battle to own the consumer" to the "cola wars". Perhaps even the use of the term "conquest", as blatant a use of imperialistic language as you could expect instead of the simple expression "get more people to use our brand": [especially loathsome when used as a verb.]

‒ I don't think I have seen brands described as being in "armed struggle" with each other, but maybe I haven't looked hard enough.

The adoption of warfare-as-way-of-life was taken to its extreme by Ries and Trout in the 1980s in their book, *Marketing Warfare*.

So what exactly is wrong with the military metaphor? Is it just a docile rhetorical trope that doesn't mean any harm to anyone? The most tenable objection to this is that metaphors are astonishingly powerful and fundamental in shaping understanding, action and thought.

The fact is that many of the most basic ideas about and practices within organizations, management and business culture are based on a relatively small number of images and metaphors that remain largely under-explored. It follows that, only by excavating the metaphor and uncovering its implicit meanings, can we hope to undo some of the damage that outdated thinking can do to our workplace lives.

So, for a start it's so, well, destructive. The language of war is filled with hierarchies, systems, the culture of "command and control" as well as being known for its generally rather aggressive and confrontational attitude to life and property.

To take the word "target" again: it implies that the "consumer" is little more than a battlefield to be fought over, and whoever has the bigger firepower and most control of their resources is likely to be victor.

Equally it is not a zero-sum game where it's "you or your enemy" and someone has to fail; business doesn't have to be like that either. Many brands effectively operate with no real competition. Or it may be the case that a victory for "our side" may be a disaster for both the environment and those carrying the enemy standard, or even the neutral population.

Then there is the fact that the semiotics of warfare reek of testosterone. Think of ads or any other form of communication for warfare, such as video games and you won't, in all likelihood, have an image of fluffy pink bunnies dressed top-to-toe in Laura Ashley floral prints.

Is it too far-fetched to ask that we cease implicitly waging a war on the consumer?

But I can't let the topic go without one final ironic twist. In these days of gaining permission, building relationships, personalizing the brand experience and building conversations and communities, **engagement** has become the poster boy for all that is good in brand and marketing communication. All that horrid talk about persuasion, all those nasty outdated models based on converting consumers via linear sequential transportation models such as AIDA: all gone and replaced by the more interactive, humanistic low involvement processing-friendly term that is "engagement".

But scratch beneath the surface of the sheep of engagement and the wolf of war is revealed: "the rules of engagement" are themselves a prize expression from the battlefield.

So even in this golden age of collaborative communication we are still at the mercy of a good old [embedded?] military metaphor.

F) SYSTEMS ARE DOING IT FOR THEMSELVES

Science itself has not remained still, stuck in the rut of reductionism, mechanism and physics envy. The boundaries between biology and physics, for example, are blurring. Thinking from evolutionary psychology, cognitive sciences and AI/A-Life to small world networks has evolved into behavioural economics which can give us new frameworks more in tune with the new broader ways of seeing the world. Let us start with the notion of networks.

One of the many pillars supporting the paradigm emerging within science is the move away from *substance* and towards *pattern and relation*. It is now (almost) common knowledge that the way we perceive our world and our place in it has changed since the impact of the cumulative insights of Darwin, Copernicus, Einstein and Heisenberg: that we are not the centre of the universe, that humans are not specially positioned in creation, and that there are forces at the microscopic level that we struggle to understand.

Old certainties about our place in the cosmos, our relationship to the rest of creation, or our grasp of the smallest and largest boundaries of our conception were shaken forcibly by their work.

First of all, many scientists have come to define our species as "pattern-makers". Take the Nobel laureate, physicist and Santa Fe complexity guru, Murray Gell-Mann, the man who coined the word "quark" after a passage in James Joyce.

He talks of people as being "complex adaptive systems (CAS)". In this way, he believes, there are universal similarities among some of the most crucial processes on earth: biological evolution, ecological systems, the mammalian immune system, the evolution of human societies and sophisticated computer software systems, to name but a few.

What links all these processes is that each relies on gathering information about itself and its interactions with its environment, building along the way a model or schema of the world around it based on regularities it perceives. So in the case of human individuals, we think, learn, use symbolic language and generate new generations of CAS in our wake (chief amongst which are powerful computers and their descendants). Later on, he adapts the term to include a CAS that acts as an interpreter and observer of the information: this he calls an Information Gathering and Utilising System (IGUS).

According to this thinking, through both our biological inheritance and our culture, we are primed to seek patterns. (See Part 2).

G) CONCLUSION: STORY HELPS US ESCAPE THE MONOCULTURE

"People think that mathematics is complicated. Mathematics is the simple bit. It's the stuff we can understand. It's cats that are complicated."

(John Conway, British mathematician and creator of Game of Life)

I hope to show that storytelling can help liberate us from the monoculture of runaway measurement and cold-hearted rationalism that is the way of the arithmocracy.

We must confront the homogenizing effects of Grayson Perry's "default man" or Duncan Watts's "representative individual", address the mechanistic monoculture of metrics and end the culture of what I call "tick-boxing" (a sport that will inevitably be introduced into any upcoming Business Olympics).

It is natural for us to look for "safety in numbers", but I worry that we have become slaves to the algorithm (witness the report that a Hong Kong venture company has appointed a machine learning programme to its board).

A culture of storytelling is a corrective check to this system that will transform our communication from being dry and derivative to something that is more persuasive, actionable and inspiring.

But how do we become storytellers?

SHORT STORY: ARE YOU RADIATOR OR DRAIN?

I once carried out a project, that required me to ask creatives what they valued from account planners. One answered with a memorable analogy. What he wanted, he responded, was a radiator not a drain: someone, who when they entered a room or made a contribution radiated thought, light and ideas. Instead, too often he got a drain: someone whose entrance drained all the life and energy from a room.

END OF PART 1

1. Our society is becoming increasingly obsessed with "arithmocracy", and in business we need to beware that we don't let scientific management or physics envy overtake the impulse for creativity and originality.

2. All of us in the branding and marketing world must ensure that the militant reductionism that has led to runaway measurement does not mean we ignore our human emotions and diversity.

3. One thing we can all do is to look beyond the dominant military metaphor that has underpinned much of the way we now do marketing.

4. A good place to start is to remind ourselves that we are biological organisms, born with an innate storytelling instinct. The arithmocracy has buried this instinct and instead replaced it with a mechanistic, reductive form of communication.

5. Now, how can we all recover and revive it?

HOW TO BECOME A STORYTELLER

Having examined the problems of living under a stern and maleficent arithmocracy, I will now attempt to prescribe how we can rebel against it under the banner of storytelling and develop a true storytelling culture.

To do this we need to start looking at some other terms that we are all used to and then determine, as we did in this first section, how we can progress beyond them.

A) **MOVING BEYOND DATA**

HELP!

"A wealth of information creates a poverty of attention."

(Herbert Simon, American political scientist and economist)

The indisputable fact is that we are all increasingly exposed to so much "information" that scientists, mathematicians and classical students are working overtime just to come up with new prefixes to put in front of "bytes", such as "exa" and "peta". New expressions are regularly being coined to describe our inability to deal with all this information: "drinking the fire hose" being one of my favourite, swimming in the same aquatic metaphor pool as "drowning in data".

Or take the term TLDNR, which has taken off in the age of email and stands for "too long, did not read"; and the acronym WWILF, for "what was I looking for?" to describe the tendency towards self-distraction while surfing the net, a phenomenon that affects two thirds of Brits online.

There is, I believe, a hierarchy or progression at work, as shown in the figure below.

LEVEL 1: DATA
At the bottom of the triangle is raw data, the oil that fuels the engine of so much of our activity within the business world. But in the narrowest sense that I want to use, it is raw, unmoulded and, in itself, of very limited utility.

Data does tend to have a bad reputation, particularly when used to stand in for statistics, and one of the reasons for the criticism is the mistake that many purveyors of data make in mistaking a catalogue for an explanation.

LEVEL 2: INFORMATION
Since humans are hunter-gatherers at heart, it is not entirely fanciful to see our age as the age of "information hunting and gathering". From the first scribes using hieroglyphics to the possession of the technology of writing in the hands of priests, information has been entangled with power, authority and control. Only relatively recently in our development has collecting, analyzing, consuming, transmitting, selling and buying become so pervasive and automatic.

There are aspects of information I want to highlight here: information as *compression*, as *surprise* and as the precursor to *meaning*.

It has been said (by media theorist Marshall Mcluhan no less) that IBM's visionary moment in the 1960s came when it discovered it was not in the business of making office machines, but of processing information. Later, with the help of the Ogilvy advertising agency, IBM moved that concept into the provision of business solutions.

Information has become data's older, smarter brother: ubiquitous, savvy and central to almost every facet of our lives. Some argue it is even the central "theory of everything" in that it has become central to so many branches of science from genetics to quantum theory to cosmology. Luciano Floridi, Professor of Philosophy of Information at Oxford, talks of people now having IT-entities, as the threshold between here (analogue, carbon-based, offline) and there (digital, silicon-based, online) becomes increasingly blurred, and the internet of things becomes ever-more embedded in our lives. We are already knee-deep in the world of what he terms "A2A [Anything to Anything]" and "A4A [Anything for Anytime]".

Information, it seems, has become the irreducible element (the etymology of atom) from which everything else grows. Evolutionary biologist and thinker Richard Dawkins is also fond of reminding us "life is just bytes and bytes of digital information."

This is essentially the heart of what we all do – or should do – especially those who work in the communications industries. We reduce facts, we simplify, we compress until the most pertinent and valuable essence is left for all to see.

To take an example: in the early Christian era, the fish symbol (sometimes known as the Jesus Fish, especially as a popular car bumper sticker) was used as code for Christians to meet at a time of Roman oppression. The choice of the fish symbol was based on its strength as an acronym, a compression of a complex idea: the Greek word for fish "Ichthus" (as in ichthyology) was chosen as each of the Greek letters of the word stood for "Jesus Christ, Son of God, Saviour". So a verbal acronym became a visual motif and a secret, shared symbol.

Danish popular science writer Tor Norretranders coined the word "exformation" to express the idea of all the material that is present in our minds or in a conversation, or in an earlier draft of information but which is not present in the final version. As he points out, how much can be safely omitted will depend very much on the context between transmitter and receiver, how much is expressly obvious to both and can therefore be readily taken for granted.

The moral I think we should draw from this is knowing what and how much is exformation: my verdict is that it is far more than we think.

So, we should always err on the side of exformation: cut out the noise to make the signal stronger, especially at the start of a presentation (See p72).

Remember that what is relatively new and exciting (information) to you is almost certainly old and mundane (exformation) to them. To put it another way, there is no surprise value in it.

B) INFORMATION AND IDEAS

Cultural historian Theodore Roszak was one of the first to insist on the priority of ideas over information, on the basis that *humans do not think in information but in ideas.*

"But information does not create ideas; by itself, it does not validate or invalidate them. An idea can only be generated, revised, or unseated by another idea........ideas come first, because ideas define, contain, and eventually produce information."

Another important preconception this challenges is that information is, in fact, essential to creating ideas. As a practitioner in the business, I have always found this particularly deeply ingrained belief hard to overturn: that, in the development of ideas, information (and even data) should be indisputably and indispensably non-negotiable ingredients.

Let me go out on a limb here: **we have to learn to break the link between data/information and ideas.**

Anyone who works in the communication, branding, sales or research worlds should heed those words. My experience has been that the majority of people still worship at the altar of "information-as-idol", without demanding to know what is the idea, goal or purpose behind that information. Its transcendent and almost gnostic power as "information" is enough, especially when shrouded by the mystique of "big data".

Most of the time, the bit *before* information is presented and – especially – the bit *after* are the most interesting times to be around.

Granted that Big Data in the age of being watched by Google can mean that data is a platform for insight and creativity, if in the right hands (or minds).

But my point is, we need to acknowledge that our assumption that originality depends on data (of whatever magnitude) is something we need to question.

If anything, information – especially in excess – acts as a barrier to creativity and the generation of ideas.

But to go back to the domain of aquatic metaphors, we are living in an industry that can be defined as DRIP ("data-rich, insight poor".)

C) **THE 'DRIP' OF SURPRISE**

Let's delve into some information theory again. One of the definitions that mathematician Claude Shannon gave for information (along with entropy, uncertainty and difficulty) was surprise. To Shannon, the amount of information was a measure of surprise, and this was related closely to probability: so surprise is the opposite of expected probability as there are more surprises in disorder than in order. A rare event, to use the rather more computational expression, is high in Shannon information.

But this "surprise value", I believe, can be translated from its rather arcane and technical domain into a more mainstream reading, and one that relates to more human changes in expectation. And this accords well with the finding central to behavioural economics that surprise is one of the six universal human emotions, alongside happiness, sadness, fear, anger and disgust.

What this means to us in a non-technical, human sense is that when we are communicating "information" be it in a presentation, a sales meeting or other situations, if we want to get a human response we must be sure to **get as much surprise out of our information as we can**. The opposite of this is to pour forth a torrent of information that has little surprise value but just reasserts what is already known.

So think: how surprised will your audience be?

Surprise is a much under-utilized tool in our business and an emotion that has been relatively poorly mined (I would say under-mined but that would mean something different).

D) INSIDE INFORMATION

The point of going back to a word's origins, just as with mining a metaphor, is to ask ourselves what are the underlying layers of nuance which the drip-drip-drip of cliché has worn away, and in so doing unearth new insights.

Whenever I run workshops or training sessions and ask people to guess the etymology I find only a few who can get beneath the rather circular answer of "to inform". Usually after a couple of digs and threats to introduce even more etymological digressions, we get to the root of the word: "form" – in the same way that "conform", "deform" "reform" or "transform" all more obviously demonstrate the notion of shape-changing, or shape-retention. As it is, or with some more Latin behind it ("shape") we can now see more clearly that our humdrum usage of "information" has been set adrift of its original and more elegant sense.

So: information, to distinguish it from the senseless onslaught of data, has form or shape. Information is best seen as the process of *adding form* or *shape*, an arrangement or moulding of something into a pre-conceived and premeditated outline and one that owes not a little to the artistic spirit.

So again, we can see some patterns emerging: that ideas are shapes or forms, and to change shapeless data into information and information into something more useful it requires a shape or an idea with a sense of a guiding vision behind it.

So, as we leave the second level that is "information" and ascend to the next tier, we do so armed with the knowledge that when we say we want to inform, we are seeking to detect, impose and ultimately communicate a form or shape and in so doing forge a relationship with and from our information.

Now: onwards and upwards.

LEVEL 3: MEANING

In the business world, information has, sadly, taken on a rather pejorative sense and this has melded with some of the Shannon-esque elements of information as mathematical transfer. What is missing and I want to emphasis here is the element of significance, of *meaning*.

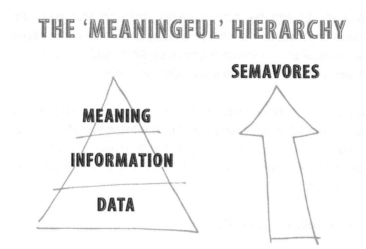

THE 'MEANINGFUL' HIERARCHY

SEMAVORES

MEANING

INFORMATION

DATA

E) **THE SEMAVORE AND THE MEANING OF MEANING**

I like to think of people as semavores. Carnivores devour meat, herbivores' chosen nutrition is vegetarian and locavores eat what is grown locally; the term semavore describes someone who seeks out and dines on meaning and significance. (The prefix sema- comes from the Greek for sign or signal and is to be found in *semantics* and one of the research industry's favourite disciplines of the moment, *semiotics*. As someone who uses semiotics in my analysis without having taken any academic courses in the subject, I often say that I am half-informed on the subject, thus putting the semi in semiotics).

And for those who cannot bear to abandon the safety of "consumer" the "eating" root might bring some solace on a dark, data-light evening.

So, let's compare the word "consumer" with "semavore". The word "consumer" has lingered for many decades, after its association with explosive post-war market growth. But, these days, it feels terribly passé and passive, bringing to mind Skinner's behaviouristic rats in a maze being observed by people in white coats carrying clipboards (today's researchers or planners, perhaps). It is at these times that I most feel like we are treating consumers as psychiatric patients in some giant social experiment by Stanley Milgram or a Derren Brown TV special.

Still worse, with the language of the market now firmly entrenched at the interactive and conversational end of the spectrum, the use of the label 'consumer' feels limited to the actions of someone largely inert and reactive.

In this context, it is also vital to separate two heavy-hitting concepts in the armoury of communication: truth and meaning.

A definition I quite admire comes from Professor of English at the University of Maryland Mark Turner's gorgeous little work, *The Literary Mind*. He reminds us, in the course of discussing the importance of parable in story, that meaning doesn't come in packets, and it is not some sort of deposit in a concept container.

"It is alive and active, dynamic and distributed, constructed for local purposes of knowing and acting."

The fact that meaning is distributed reminds us of the sciences of complexity we have mentioned before: meaning emerges, is constructed and refined almost ceaselessly. Meaning links.

So, for brands, we must go against much of the orthodoxy and search primarily for brand *meanings* not brand *truths*: truth implies fixity, rigidity as well as incontestable verity. Anyone involved in brand positioning, or who has worked to devise a brand or creative pitch, acknowledges that there are always "many ways to skin the brand cat" precisely because there are few brands where there is only one absolute truth or singular meaning.

One of my personal rants is about trying to subsume a brand (or a creative brief) into one benefit or message. So many brands these days are polyvalent, offering a range of different benefits and experiences. Think of a holiday destination like the Bahamas, or a product such as the Apple iPad or the Dyson Airblade hand-dryer. To take the Dyson: it is faster, more hygienic, less wasteful, less noisy and more ecologically friendly on several counts. How to reduce this to one expression?

Yet brand owners too often insist on using the term "brand truth" as if that is The Word, The One True Message that must be communicated. It brings with it a whole cargo of assumptions: that the truth is invariably a rational attribute, and that it can be conveyed in communication in a rational manner that is susceptible to traditional tools of research measurement.

F) THE MEANING MODEL

Those of us who communicate brands need to stop looking for messages and truth and concentrate on meaning. This is especially the case for brands: if culture is the common heritage of shared meaning and collective imagination, then a company should aim to become a "meaning broker".

The users of a brand can best be seen as a "community of interpretation", and a brand itself I would describe as a "tribe of shared meaning". This assumes that people (semavores) share a desire for a brand that is not so much based on a fact or benefit of a brand, but the values and meanings that it espouses.

The new thinking about aggregated behaviour confirms this change of perspective.

MODEL	Communication	"Consumer"	Company	Brand	Planner	Researcher
OLD	Messaging	Passive targets	Vendor	Attribute	Voice of brand, conscience of "consumer"	Interrogator
NEW	Feeder of Meaning	Meaning-seeking semavores	Meaning-making rights owner	Tribe of shared meaning	Keeper of meaning	Meaning-hunter

BARNEY THE DINOSAUR

It may not be universally appreciated that Barney the Purple Dinosaur is in flagrant contravention of the Geneva Convention of Human Rights.

It emerged that the US Psychological Operation department (Psy Ops) was using specific genres of music to try and break the will of detainees in Iraq. This form of audio interrogation was based on evidence that some captives were being forced to stay awake for up to four days listening to loud music. (This is also a by-product of living in several parts of London).

But as well as more expected genres and bands, such as "death metal" and Metallica, the Barney song *I Love You* was chosen for its capacity to inflict unbearable torture on listeners through mindless repetition (with an added risk of saccharine poisoning). In the torture trade, this is known as "futility music" in that it is designed to make you feel that maintaining your position is pointless. I prefer to think that several choruses of "I love you, you love me, we're a happy family" is enough to intimidate the sanest of humans into believing that life itself is futile.

In early 2009, authorities in Christchurch, New Zealand hit on a similar idea when they needed to rid the town centre of unwanted punks: they chose to blast out Barry Manilow songs.

Though to be clear, the Central City Business Association manager Paul Lonsdale did inform journalists, "I did not say Barry Manilow is a weapon of mass destruction".

An advertising equivalent is the Cillit Bang campaign in the UK, featuring an actor screaming "Hi, I'm Barry Scott". The Reckitt Benckiser brand achieved unexpected saliency and success having being introduced to the UK in 2004 after a Hungarian launch.

In a spirit of post-modern relativism, this garish, infomercial approach was quite successful among many who saw it as a spearhead for a new no-nonsense authenticity. Do watch and savour one of the many remixes.

G) HOW TO BECOME A PATTERN-TATE

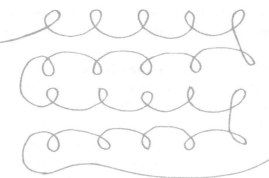

"I link therefore I am."

(SJ Singer, biologist – his take on Descartes)

Semavores are hopelessly devoted to the search for pattern and order, as well as meaning.

All organisms are pattern-extractors that depend on seeking order over chaos for their survival.

Not only are we devourers of meaning, but I'd like to suggest we are also "pattern-tates", because we gain power through pattern.

In the same way that our brains detect patterns in the visual forms of nature and in sound, they naturally hunt out patterns in information. One example is stories: stories provide recognizable patterns and in those patterns we find meaning.

An absence of pattern can send us into chaos and distress. As a keen skier, I find a "white out" can be quite traumatic and disorientating: an information white out can have similar effects.

WHY WE ARE NATURAL PATTERN-FINDERS

There has been a recent outpouring of evidence from the worshipful tribe of behavioural economists highlighting our systemic irrationality both in terms of our dependence on our emotions for decision-making, and our relative weakness in the face of large numbers, probability and logic. I will use the terms popularized by "the most important psychologist alive today", as Steven Pinker labelled Daniel Kahneman.

Our System 1 operates instinctively as the pattern-finding mechanism and carries this out beneath the threshold of consciousness, meaning that often patterns are found and connections are made without the knowledge (or approval) of the more deliberative and rational System 2.

One instance of this is our tendency to devise and rely on heuristics. These are mental short-cuts, derived from the Greek verb "to find": the same root is behind Archimedes's famous in-bath exclamation "Eureka!" or "I have found it" ("it" being an original theory of displacement rather than an errant rubber duck).

Heuristics are a driving force behind more of our behaviour and decision-making than we would like to admit. Sometimes called cognitive biases, they are click-whirr processes that lead us to follow certain paths that have worked for us in the past (so why shouldn't they work for us again now?). They are the brain's auto-pilot: efficient and easy, fast and frugal and they save the brain from having to deliberate at length over every single decision that it encounters, an impossible demand for our most energy-hungry organ.

They have been designed by natural selection to enable us to survive and thrive, and probably originated with a process based on searching the environment to decide which of the four "F-actions" we should carry out: flee, fight, feed or mate.

A LITTLE BIT (BUT NOT TOO MUCH) ON SATISFICING

Part of the behavioural economics worldview is the acceptance that "satisficing" is a common behavioural *modus* operandi for most human beings. Psychologist Barry Schwartz's bestselling book, *The Paradox Of Choice* demonstrated that not only does much decision-making not make us happy, but that it is a consideration that those of us in the influencing business should give more attention to when we are trying to understand how to modify someone's decision or gain their attention.

Schwartz starts from the premise that nowadays, for most of us, there are simply too many choices. We are sinking in a sea of super-abundant information and choice: there are approximately 700 breakfast cereals in the UK, 180,000 registered charities, and more than 75 billion cookbooks published every second.

(OK, that isn't quite exact. But TV chef Jamie Oliver's *30 Minute Meals* broke the record as the fastest-selling non-fiction book of all time, shifting 735,000 copies in 10 weeks and going on to sell over 1.2 million copies in the UK.)

The default assumption of many of the people dedicated to selling their brand, service or self is still that more information and more choice is good, as long as it's their brand that is chosen, of course.

But, a combination of common sense and behavioural economics suggests otherwise. Unless we are the most dedicated choice junkies unlimited by constraints, how could we possibly have the time, let alone the energy or mental capacity, to make reasoned, empirical choices that would make us happy at every choice juncture?

Schwartz argues that people he terms "maximizers" – people who obsess about the details of every decision until they have optimized their decision – are likely to be less happy than "satisficers", who settle for a decision that is *good enough.*

The question we have to ask ourselves is: Are we treating our audience as maximizers, devoted to our every chart and word, or are they more likely to be satisficers, who want an efficient answer that doesn't make undue demands on their time or attention?

WHEN PATTERN GOES WRONG

Finally, let us look at the phenomenon known as "pareidolia" (singular: pareidolion, meaning "wrong image"), a part of the tendency to invest random noise with pattern and meaning.

The fact that so many of them are seen as religious or spiritual (see the notes for a list of examples from YouTube) shows that we most look for meaning where we need it: hence the preponderance of "Mother Teresa in a bun" examples (the amusingly-titled *Nun Bun*) and so many that appear to be of Jesus. Part of this tendency is undoubtedly anthropomorphic: we see ourselves in everything, such as "the man in the moon" or UFO sightings and aliens, an insight that goes back at least as far as David Hume. It is also a by-product of our evolutionary tendency to look for faces in everything, even in the simplest line drawings, something that has been noted in infants.

Sometimes, we just have to accept that the fact that "Presbyterians" is an anagram of "Britney Spears" is of no meaning at all.

But in this last leg of our journey, it is the pattern-seeking instinct that opens the door into storytelling.

END OF PART 2

1. We can start on the path to becoming storytellers, by appreciating that we were not designed by evolution to decipher spreadsheets or find enrichment in PowerPoint.

2. Our industry, flooded by the sea of big data, is now DRIP: data-rich, insight poor.

3. To create insight and meaning, we should see ourselves, our audiences and our consumers as Semavores, who seek out meaning.

4. So aim to create meaning in your communication, rather than assume that data or information is enough.

5. Part of telling a story is to realize how much needs to be omitted; so ensure you maximize your exformation.

6. Remember that inside information is the word "form": so always find shape for your data.

7. Ideas don't need information: are you brave enough to break the dependence on information?

TOP TIPS FOR STORYTELLING

TIP 1: **THE TRANS FACTS**

Latin words that have a "trans" prefix all have the same root meaning, literally "across".

So I think that, in our search for ways to counter the arithmocracy and bring meaning back to business communication, these trans-words are a good declaration of intent for our mission. And I promise they will be better for you than trans-fats. So let's get you saturated.

TRANSFORM
As we have seen, the goal of storytelling in our commercial environment should be to change the form, pattern and structure of our audience's world, their expectations, and ideally, their behaviour.

Earlier, we saw the importance of form and pattern and how the brain craves it at almost any expense.

If we have not changed the mental structures of our audience (or in some cases reinforced them) we have failed. We will have simply added to their data freight and added no meaning, value, insight or legacy.

Communication by story should be designed to change the shape of the data or information that we have to bestow, or to create a new shape where only formlessness existed before. Have we made something clear, given it a shape for the first time in our audience's head?

There is much talk in the industry of and demand for "transformative" or "transformational" ideas and insights. Storytelling has been under our noses for centuries and we have neglected its power to change the shape of the way we think and structure information.

To "transform" emphasizes pattern and shape. We are business communications transformers.

TRANSLATE

It is often said that translation is one of the defining human characteristics.

I want to separate "translate" and "transport" by giving "transport" a more emotional hue. As a linguistic exercise, it is key to our ability to share meaning across different cultures and domains.

As all language mavens would confirm, metaphor is key to human thought, a concept that adds enrichment to language as well as being essential to making abstract information easier to grasp and process. Steven Pinker, who knows a thing or two about language, has even described language as being a mix of metaphor and combinatorics (the power of permutation to create almost infinite novelty). It is a bridge from the unfamiliar to the familiar.

Metaphor-mapping and analogy are undoubted tools in the armoury of cognition and the priests of persuasion in the advertising industry and spin medicine acknowledge its efficacy. Lakoff goes as far as to say that frames even trump facts and we are all too often enslaved by a good metaphor, before we have thought it through.

A good metaphor can be a new frame, a fresh lens through which to view the world, a political party or a brand. It is a shame that most commercial presentations and attempts at persuasion fail to deliver in the same way. What does this mean for us as storytellers?

First, if we are presenting research data or information, we must remember that we are translating for an audience and our language may well be different from theirs. As translators, we must ask ourselves:

1. Do we appreciate the difference between our "language" and the language of our audience? In some cases this will be linguistic; more often it will also be cultural or commercial.
2. So we may have to take a creative, cultural or linguistic leap to ensure that we are not stuck in our original language (data, cliché, verbatim reporting of "consumer" speak from research, acronym-crammed technical specification and the rest).
3. Specifically, this means that we must always look to translate "up".

By this I mean moving from the specific, the particular and the individual to the general, the rational to the emotional, universal and the insightful.

In our search for meaning, or the dissemination of it for other semavores, we should always be looking for higher-level abstractions, principles and laws.

TRANSPORTATION

In the world of communication theory in which I grew up, this was the generic term for all those theories that emphasized the linear-sequential view of human decision-making.

They all had, at their core, a belief that there were various stages of behaviour that consumers went through (in an approved and defined sequence) culminating in the marketer's holy grail of purchase.

Generally, they were along the following lines:
Awareness/attention
Interest
Desire
Action

These models have been largely discredited by developments in psychology, neuroscience and the recent [tidal] wave of behavioural economics, which as we have seen, emphasize that decisions are more non-linear, unconscious and context-dependent than these old models suggest. Sadly, because they are so linear, rational and safe these decrepit models still offer the veneer of a safety net to some.

But let's look at the other connotation of "transport". The feeling of being carried away and transported to other lands, other lives, the sense we get when we are interrupted by our destination, or a family member in the midst of a compelling drama or a crucial football match.

The emotions or moods in question are in the area of awe and transcendent otherness. In the literature of emotion, it is linked to the "oceanic feeling", of uplifting bliss and an almost mystical intensity: for many it is exactly what they experience as a religious or spiritual revelation.

There is indeed a "psychological theory of transportation" according to which becoming immersed in a story has powerful emotional and (note) persuasive effects. In this context, when focused on narrative, attention, imagery and feelings work together in this immersive state to create responses that are "participatory".

Transportation has been at the heart of every new medium. Some theorists argue that every new channel – oral, written, visual, all the way to the net and gaming – has increased the transformative and "transportative" power of storytelling too.

Again returning to the ancient roots of language, motion and emotion both operate in the same sphere: of movement. We still talk metaphorically of being "moved".

Some experts use the term "elevation", which seems to be linked to the release of oxytocin.

The "elevator pitch" perhaps should be re-cast as the "elevation pitch", a summary of our thinking or presentation which creates a sense of wonder, awe and inspiration.

So we should be asking ourselves how we intend to create even the merest hint of that transportation in the world of meetings, face-to-face sessions, brainstorms, debrief and conference calls. Where do we want to take our audience from and to?

Here is Simon Hattenstone, *Guardian* journalist, features writer and interviewer:

"What stories have you got? Have you got a great story? Because you can have the most interesting story and you can still bore them to death. If someone can spend 90 minutes talking to you and you can't summarize what you've heard, they've failed. It's not enough to ramble incoherently."

TIP 2: MASSAGE NOT MESSAGE

It has long been recognized, at least intuitively by planners in advertising agencies and the more thoughtful ad researchers, that the messaging model of communication has been left in place way past its "message by" date. It depended on the traditional rational, behaviouristic transportation theory of information relay which deals in information rather than meaning.

So, I would like to offer another maxim, one that would also make a damn fine T-shirtable slogan: "*Massage Not Message*".

The heart of our communication, be it advertising to consumers, presenting to the BIGs [our Bosses in Geneva], or selling in the new resized pack format to the trade, should be about massaging the ego and self-worth of our audience rather than the informational content of what we have to say.

Yes, that runs counter to much of what we have been taught, or absorbed from books and courses on Marcomms and *A Hundred Ways To Make Charts and Bore People*; but the human truth, one that works from semavores to semavores is that the primary aim should be to understand how to affect human feeling and behaviour.

Rather irritatingly, evolutionary psychologist Geoffrey Miller has already come up with a word to define our dependence on and calculation of our status: "status-ticians".

In the light of our need to signal our fitness indicators, it should surprise nobody that we are constantly in a process of emitting and receiving signals in our desire to display desirable traits in the pursuit of fitness-promotion.

Storytellers over the ages have been able to carry out strategic trait-signalling by displaying their talent for story, to focus attention, to intrigue, surprise, entertain and instruct. Today's great storytellers can command an audience, hold a stage and thereby earn our reward and approval.

This is not to say that manipulation, flattery and sycophancy are the chief ingredients in the business world, but rather we would be far wiser to heed the foundational insights of communications theory: that of understanding what people want, rather then telling them what we have.

In this sense it is plausible to see our beliefs in the same way as our memories, as being almost like possessions, but even more than badges or emblems they are the armature of our identity and self.

This brings us back to the universal human need for flattery and ego massage. Another dip into the stream of etymology will serve us well. Because behind the word "belief" is a complex of meanings. Behind the Old English geleafa "belief, faith", we can just spot *galaub- "dear, esteemed," from intensive prefix *ga- + *leubh- meaning "to care, desire and love." It is thus cognate with "liebe" in modern German and Latin "libido".

So rather than relying on truth, fact, information and other quantities we have been dissecting since Part 1, belief is revealed to depend on the most universal and hard-wired instinct of all (barring survival), namely love.

To believe is to love, to invest an emotional response in something rather than impartially accept one truth from among all the competing truths.

TIP 3: PAY ATTENTION TO ATTENTION

The perils of infocopia have been examined already. We are surrounded on all sides by an arithmocracy that excretes steaming [or, digitally, *streaming*] piles of data, which besiege our embattled attention (note deliberate military metaphor).

Commentators have rushed to examine the war on attention (I'm stopping, I promise) from both sides.

[Not *the*] Neil Young, the former executive of gaming giant, Electronic Arts, wrote of our tendency to "additive comprehension", where, in transmedia storytelling, additional details can add richer layers from one medium of a story. I would prefer to misinterpret the expression and use "*addictive* comprehension", which I would then define as the insistent and compulsive urge to explore more and more of what we deem worthy of our focus. Note to communicators: this is not necessarily what you want people to be "engaging with", such as your brand or its new social media idea.

Media theorist Henry Jenkins expressed this as: *"If you give people enough to explore, they will explore"*.

My favourite term is what former Apple and Microsoft visionary, Linda Stone, called CPA or *continuous partial attention*. This adorable expression sums up beautifully the challenge (or curse) of always-on-multi-media and the ease with which we find that we can be simultaneously multi-preoccupied. Yet, of course, this divided attention means that we are never fully focused on one area, but divided, segmented, disturbed and distracted. We are constantly scanning the environment for what is more important than what is happening, what is more related to our sense of self-worth and validation.

Stone distinguishes CPA from multi-tasking by suggesting that CPA is more about never wanting to feel like we are missing something rather than just the simple goal of being more productive. The US Air Force prefers the term "task saturation" to describe the potentially silent killer that can affect performance, as you start to crack and then panic. As "components within the aviation system", one report helpfully notes, task-saturated people are dangerous. In the US Air Force, it is called "dying relaxed".

SEMI—DETACHED BOX

In fact in a similar spirit to Stone, I would like to proffer my own humble addition to the ranks of zeitgeist acronyms to describe the assault on what I can barely bring myself to call "our bandwidth": SEMI.

This can stand for any or all of the following:
- Someone Else More Important
- Something Else More Important
- Someone Else More Interesting
- Something Else More Interesting

So when we are listening to a presentation, much of our attention (conscious or otherwise) is in SEMI mode.

So next time you think about putting up that chart called *Spontaneous Brand Opinion of All Luxury Cars in Japan By Number of Models Aware 2008-2013* just reflect that it is, in fact, a signal for SEMI to kick in and for the sufferer to scan their smartphone, check their calendar or ponder whether they would play Rooney upfront or in the hole.

Philosopher, poet and novelist Raymond Tallis, author of *The Kingdom of Infinite Space* has coined the word "e-tennuation", which he has defined as the condition whereby:

"....people find it increasingly difficult to be here now rather than dissipating themselves into an endless electronic elsewhere."

In other writing, he has talked of it as *"a kind of existential numbness. The hollowing of presence by e-sense."*

We saw earlier the slightly less erudite acronym WWILF, which stands for "what was I looking for?" a label to describe aimless surfing, and I think there is something very disorderly, dishevelled and System 1 about this.

Opinion about the implications of all this attention-divisiveness is, well, divided, with science writer and theorist Steven Johnson in the pro corner and technology writer Nicholas *"The Shallows"* Carr opposing vehemently. Our friends in the magic business and the neuroscientists are aware of the phenomenon known as misdirection or "inattentional blindness". This happens when conspicuous events within a scene are missed while observers focus on (or are misdirected towards) an irrelevant task. This illusion of attention has been famously demonstrated in the video where you are required to count the number of basketball passes being made (I prefer not to give the title of the video as it is effectively a spoiler). Suffice to say that about half the subjects in the experiment fail to notice the "elephant" in the room.

There is a fabulous scientific deconstruction of this process full of insights, magical, a-has and false endings, devised by Professor of Psychology, magician and all round good guy Richard Wiseman, called the "Amazing Colour Change Card Trick". I defy you not to be amazed.

So what does this say about storytelling and its potential?

Hands up who thinks that what we all need in this era of SEMI-CPA-Distraction is an app that allows you to indulge in some self-distractive behaviour?

Well the App Genie has granted your wish. Fred Stuzman, a researcher at Carnegie Mellon University's Heinz College has created a number of apps to force you to focus and not go into blind auto-distract mode. One app, tellingly called Freedom, enables you to lock yourself out of your internet connection for a set time, until you reboot. Try Freedom for only $10, it proclaims, highlighting how the likes of Naomi Klein, Dave Eggers and Nick Hornby have got great value and even greater productivity for their 10 bucks.

Another milder version, Anti-Social, merely prevents you from accessing social media sites.

That above all, we need to create and maintain focus, and avert the threat of distraction or inattentional blindness to what we are saying, writing or presenting. Too often, we assume that the blizzard of detail we are offering will automatically create focus and attract attention, especially if it is accompanied by oodles of sincerity and some nice infographics.

But if we do, we underestimate the extent to which our victims will easily and inexorably lead themselves to consider something which is more pertinent to their sense of self. Maybe rather than getting a TLDNR (too long, did not read) beware that you might be getting a TBDNC: too boring did not care.

TIP 4: BE GOSSIP WORTHY

"The purpose and joy of gossip is to strengthen community norms through essentially dramatic discourse."

(David Mamet, American playwright, essayist, screenwriter and film director)

"Conversation is king. Content is just something to talk about."

(Cory Doctorow, Canadian-British blogger, journalist and author)

According to Professor Robin Dunbar, who has perhaps done most to deserve the honorific "King of Gossip" (Perez Hilton excepted) approximately two-thirds of all human communication is gossip about oneself or others.

The debate among scientists as to the origin of the "runaway brain" and the sudden growth in human language development has generated many exciting and provocative theories. Dunbar believes that gossip was at the heart of it:

1. Physical grooming was a key element in social organization:
   - It reduces stress, is pleasurable for groomer and groomed and needs investment of time
   - So it is key in bonding groups of individuals to oil the wheels of social interaction
2. Language, Dunbar argues, evolved into an ultra-efficient way of grooming and, as such, is a good candidate for explaining the explosive evolution of language in our species
   - It began to replace grooming and facilitated the bonding of larger groups through the exchange of social information.

Why have we not given greater attention to the importance of gossip? I suspect it is because of our sense of inflated dignity and status as homo sapiens: we can't be that wise if we spend so much time "gossiping" surely?

TALKING UP GOSSIP
But the very informality of gossip has given it a bad press and especially so in the buttoned-up, puritanical arithmocracy of modern-day business.

The communications industry has developed a range of sophisticated ways of repositioning, reframing, upgrading and revalorizing gossip. It has been searching through the thesaurus for ways of disguising the fact that, as Doctorow suggests, content is really only there to fuel conversation; that is, gossip. Buzzy brand words of the moment such as "momentum", "energy", "advocacy" and "word-of-mouth" all pay due deference to this fact: that most communication, including marketing communication, is a form of language, and that language is used as much for gossip as it is for information.

Gossip, if we are honest, is just news with bad PR.

A rapid scoot through the role that gossip plays would suggest a plethora of roles, including:

- Vocal grooming: social anthropologist Kate Fox's term to cover the corresponding way we use gossip to navigate social relationships in the way other primates use physical grooming to reduce stress and release endorphins.
- A boundary-setter for society, in that it provides the channel for "in-groups" – groups that we are part of – to stay "in-groups". In that sense, it has a didactic and moral role, as well as acting as law-enforcer and teacher. Gossip builds and reinforces communities, in the way that brands can.
- As such, it conveys the power and prestige of status, and plays a part in impression management: guess what I know (and you don't) and guess who you heard it from first? As Tip 2 showed, most communication is not primarily about the exchange of information or truth telling: it is more about conveying an impression.

INFORMATION, GOSSIP AND BRANDS
So, gossip is linked to information, and mainly in the sense of transmission of socially useful information that confers status.

Gossip is why mobile phones have become an indispensable tool in the armoury of youth and why it is socially inappropriate for anyone over 28 to pretend they are "cool". A recent Mintel report claimed that twice as many kids aged two-to-five years old can play with a smartphone application as tie their own shoelaces.

The marketing world has taken its time to show its interest in "conversational marketing" and the discovery that word of mouth is the most powerful (and effective) tool to propagate ideas. The burgeoning of social media is testament to the timeless power of our need to swap gossip. What used to be sitting around a campfire is now using 140 characters on Twitter. Same universal human need, different channel.

The fact that some commentators come over all snooty and high-minded about the mindlessness of social media misses the point completely.

When we present, communicate and seek to persuade we would do well to frame this in terms of *"how can we create gossip based on what we have to say?"*

Nobel prize-winning psychologist Daniel Kahneman, whom we met earlier, has even admitted that one of the aims of his magisterial book *Thinking Fast and Slow* was to get people discussing his ideas around the water cooler. "I wrote this book", he claimed, "to educate gossip."

TIP 5: DO IT IN STYLE

Style has been described as the ability to express the greatest number of ideas in the fewest number of words.

Seek to make this your goal.

If we look at how language itself has evolved and the reasons for that, we can see three forces at work: economy, expressiveness and analogy.

Economy has led to the contraction of expressions and words to speed efficiency of understanding. This is why, in French, the month of Augustus became Août, why the old Saxon "hlaf-weard" [meaning bread warden] became "lord" and hlæfdige [dough-kneader] turned into "lady". The Italian "ciao" by the same process was descended form "schiavo vostro" ("your slave").

In the same way, meanings as well as words, are prone to erosion, which is why words like *terrific, fabulous* and (most currently, especially if you are in the US and under 30) *awesome* have become but weak shadows of their original selves. The parallel in business speak? The way in which words and expressions like "intense indulgence", "treat", "fashion forward" and "personal productivity" lose their meaning after repeated exposure. So, always aim for economy of expression and compression of content.

The other two forces are *expressiveness*, the need to push our ability to express ourselves in ever more original and striking ways, and analogy, which we have already covered especially under the guise of metaphor.

Part of the way we can best deploy language is the strict avoidance of cliché. As we have seen throughout, language is a powerful tool that is constantly taken for granted and eroded through banal nature of repetition.

Here, based on my own sad experience as both perpetrator and victim, is a brief selection of what to avoid:

- Iconic images that were powerful decades ago such as that one of Albert Einstein sticking out his tongue. I once worked on a major software brand, Lotus, and both agency and client concurred on only one creative mandatory: no pictures of Einstein, the brain or Einstein's brain.
- *[The brain one is especially tough now that neuroscience seeps through most planners' presentations, especially at conferences.]*
- Any use of the word "icon" unless it's specifically referring to a religious artefact.
- Anything relating to Picasso.
- Most quotations from Oscar Wilde.
- Maslow's pyramid [sorry, triangle]. Trust me, you need a really good reason to use it.
- Marketing clichés as pictures: the super tanker, the iceberg (where the most important stuff is beneath the surface) and circles, be they virtuous, vicious or morally neutral.
- Darwin, since he has become the go-to-guy for anything that needs to be said that suggests change. But as a personal favourite of mine I find this a hard one to proscribe. So we'll let him survive.....
- ......but not "evolutionary rather than revolutionary", which has become an empty vessel, meaning little more than "slow".

Here is a chart I use to highlight the tendency of too many presentations to trade in visual cliché (it's a triangle masquerading as a pyramid to add unjustifiable depth to what I'm saying) and to cram in as many words as possible into small a space (one chart).

THE SPEWED LITANY
OF INERT FACTOIDS

Essence
One of a select
group of about
13 words

CORE VALUES (3 only)
Data   More Data   Another bit

What's the personality
Like Apple, please
Masculine Yet Strangely Feminine
...Oh, and innocent

**HOW DOES This Brief
MAKE ME FEEL**

Dead inside

Not really creative

**WHAT DOES WRITING
THIS SAY ABOUT ME**

I have a larger mortgage
than I should have

I want to keep my job

**WHAT ARE THE FACTS, TRUTHS,
LEGENDS & ICONS**

Branson, Jobs, Roddick, Einstein,
You Get The Idea

**WHAT ARE PHYSICAL
REWARDS**

Blah Blah Blah

Client Facts   ASA stuff

Anything to get Account Man off my back

At all costs, force yourself not to default to that image of a key, onion, triangle-aspiring-to-be-pyramid, pillar, or anything else that tries to reduce something as messy and complicated as a brand (or a "consumer") into a regulation one size-fits-all model.

This chart makes one other point too: we have become institutionally lazy around brand and comms language. Too often, the dictates of the arithmocracy and the need to standardize a set of words (or rules) that keeps Geneva and Dallas happy, means we end up with something that is too neutral and dry to work with, the language of the lowest-common-denominator.

How often have you seen (or helped create) a series of words for the "brand personality" or the proposition that could fit a hundred other such examples? How often does your company or brand want to be seen as "just like" Apple, Innocent, Prêt a Manger, IKEA or Zara?

Recently I heard that the UK television broadcaster Channel 4 used the word "mischief" as part of its vision.

What a brilliant word that is. In the first place, it brings with it the sense of risk and naughtiness, a trait that too many brand owners would have used research to undermine on the basis that it might be too "risky", with its undercurrent of misbehaviour and trouble-making. But that is precisely the space that Channel 4 has made its own in editorial and entertainment terms, and respect is due to it for integrating that term into everything it does rather than trying to adopt or adapt some existing terminology ("we are passionate about our consumers") from another brand. Try and use memorable language, create new coinages of the realm if you can.

One famous example of science's predilection for a compact neologism is "the Big Bang". When astronomer Fred Hoyle coined the term in 1949, he intended to mock the idea. However, it caught on and much to his annoyance became the popular expression for the theory. So much so that he later said:

"Words are like harpoons. Once they go in, they are very hard to pull out."

Finally, remember the words of novelist Martin Amis. In one of his essays, he says that all writing is a "campaign against cliché". The path to cliché avoidance? Write with "freshness, energy and reverberation of voice". This is a challenge, but one that will ensure you resonate or echo ("reverberate") once you have left your stage.

TIP 6: FROM ARISTOTLE TO ELP

ETHOS

After a musical education of the Beatles and Roxy Music, I dabbled a little with the so-called progressive rock bands of the early 1970s. Chief among these was ELP, Emerson Lake and Palmer, famed, among other things, for their extravagant synthesizer solos, complex time signatures, adaptations of work by the likes of composer Aaron Copeland and poet William Blake and an overweening pomp and grandiosity that punk rock would come along and find all too easy to dismiss with a sneer and a spit.

Some 2,320 years earlier, Greek philosopher Aristotle had something to say about ELP, but was referring to something other than extended synthesizer solos, though some classical scholars argue that this may appear in one of his many lost works.

Among his voluminous writings, he wrote on rhetoric and persuasion and identified three characteristics in the art of persuasive rhetoric: ethos, logos and pathos.

These can still serve us well.

a) Ethos
By ethos, Aristotle meant what we would now call trust, credibility or authority. In modern terms, that means ensuring that you and your story have an internal sense of coherence and believability, and that

everything surrounding it shares the same integrity. One might go as far as to suggest that "ethos" is the Aristotelian equivalent of brand character or identity.

One early example of the appeal to ethos is Mark Antony's speech at the funeral of Julius Caesar, which begins "Friends, Romans, Countrymen, lend me your ears."

This also tallies with the emergence of authenticity in modern business branding. By authenticity, I mean what is natural, creative, quirky, original and distinctive. The synthetic, on the other hand, can be classified as all surface, manu-fake-ture and cheesy. The authentic has been harnessed for Budweiser's "True" campaign, the Dove campaign for real beauty and Carlo Petrini's "Slow Food Nation"; also, arguably, Danny Boyle's distinctive retelling of recent British history at the opening ceremony of the London 2012 Olympics.

An area with which I am more than familiar is that of travel and tourism, and the issue of ethos as authenticity is one that currently concerns that sector.

"[Authenticity] is a buzzword these days," says Zachary Rabinor, owner of Journey Mexico, a Puerto Vallarta-based DMC that partners with Virtuoso.

"My challenge is injecting a traveller's experience with real interactions and doing that with integrity."

A recent World Travel Market Global Trends report included 10 uses of the word "authentic" and, after "natural beauty", authenticity was deemed the second most important factor in choosing a holiday destination according to FutureBrand's Country Brand Index.

To take a couple of examples of authenticity, from both ends of the spectrum, there is a project in Paris, France, called la Périféerique. This is a self-proclaimed "mad and serious" project to open up the peripherique (the orbital route around Paris) for one day a year to pedestrians, sports fans and other environmental campaigners. There is also a play on the fanciful folly of the idea with the pun "féerique" meaning "fairy-like" in French.

At the other end of the authenticity spectrum (the home of the epic fail) are two examples: one of borrowed authenticity, and one where it was wrenched away from its owners and left to struggle for itself.

The first is an example which occurred to one of my clients, the UK office of the Bahamas Tourist Office.

A couple of years ago, while those of us working on the Bahamas Tourism Office account in the UK were minding our own strategic business and concentrating on letting the people of the Bahamas tell their own stories to attract British tourists, we came across an ad for the Costa Brava in Spain, headlined "Where does the Costa Brava start?" The main picture for the ad, sourced from Getty Images, turned out to be from.....The Bahamas. In fact it was from the world-renowned pink-sand beach on Harbour Island (due disclosure: I have trodden on its sand and it is both pink and glorious), and the Spanish tourist office both admitted that it was not actually from their coast and – to exacerbate things – that they had to dull the colour of the sand digitally to make it appear closer to the colour of the sand in the area of Costa Brava. The local director of tourism didn't seem especially repentant:

"But when we came to make the advert we didn't have the adequate images with sufficient quality," she admitted to Spanish media.

My Bahamian clients felt a mixture of pride and amusement, schadenfreude not being an especially Bahamian term or trait.

But this pales into Costa Bravian paleness in comparison with the saga of Britain's "Fake Lapland". A theme park in the Dorset/Hampshire borders was recently created offering a "magical festive experience" and a "bustling Christmas market" for all the family. However, delivery failed to live up to promise and instead of a market there were two isolated stalls selling German sausages and a selection of turkey or pork baguettes; the "magical tunnel of light" turned out to be a set of fairy lights strung across some trees, the nativity scene was set on a billboard, and smoking Santas and some bored-looking huskies sat around in a muddy field added to the sense of under-fulfillment.

Within days of opening and an (unseasonable) roasting from the gleeful UK media, trading standards officials had received thousands of complaints as reports came in of one of the elves being "smacked in the face and pushed into a pram".

A spokesman for Dorset Council explained:

"I've heard of someone spending £3,000 on tickets and terrible stories of real human misery."

Which seems something of an exaggeration in the larger scale of the human condition. But this is what happens when ethos goes wrong.

Why are we so attuned to looking out for trust and ethos?

Experts on personality discrimination have discerned what are known as the "big five personality dimensions". The five-factor model believes in stable and enduring individual characteristics, though we may all have each in varying degrees. The five are usually referred to via the acronym OCEAN: openness, conscientiousness, extraversion, agreeableness and neuroticism.

Here I just want to concentrate on the fact that one of the key questions we find ourselves asking each other in personal or professional contexts, is: are you reliable? Put another way, can I trust you? These questions will be answered by our background, our class, even our credit ratings but also how we can present ourselves.

This round of questioning seems to be a search for indicators of conscientiousness. This is the biological basis for what Aristotle would have called "ethos".

Ethos- trust or authority- will come if we have complete control over our material

LOGOS
In the beginning was the word, or "logos" in Greek, the root of all of our "-ology" words in English as well as all things "logical". What Aristotle and the Classical Greek authors meant by logos was straightforward and is covered by previous chapters on messaging: rational persuasion by the use of argument and appeal to human rationality.

The Greeks – who loved a good contrast – would compare logos to pathos, rationality to emotion. Take Euripides's play, *The Bacchae* where the god of fertility and wine, Dionysus, is set against Pentheus, King of Thebes, in a duel of heart versus head. In that play, it was emotion that triumphed spectacularly and savagely.

But more broadly, the Greeks feared that the sophists' oratory could "make the weaker argument stronger" in any situation.

PATHOS
Pathos is the appeal to the emotions of an audience and has at its etymological heart the word for "experience" or "suffer", which we still see buried underneath pathological, pathetic, empathetic, sympathetic and even (via Latin) patient.

One of the central tenets of the behavioural economics enterprise has been to insist on the centrality of human emotions in human behaviour, and especially in decision-making, against the decades of hegemony of the "homo economicus" model which asserted that we are only interested in maximizing our own utility on purely rational grounds. For many years I have been running training sessions to emphasize the errors of this model.

Work that derives ultimately from Charles Darwin, and later through Paul Ekman, shows that emotional instincts are universally hardwired into us all.

The reason (as it were) why it is so important in business communication to acknowledge the primacy of emotion is:
- To demonstrate, unequivocally, that emotions have far more sway in our decisions than we like to think
- To dispel certain long-held myths about how people make decisions

- To show how when we write about people and purchasing, we need to think, write and hypothesize more emotionally
- To help create deeper brand and communications insights via a deeper understanding of the role of emotion and influence
- To remind us that in writing research questions we must dig deeper
- To create new models/mechanisms/clues as to how to get at emotional drives and what I call universal human truths (UHTs).

I have always felt that the reason why it has taken so long for the primacy of emotion to take root in the business world is because it offends against the arithmocracy, with their belief in the divine infallibility of numbers and the belief that dates back to our friend Aristotle that "man is a rational animal" and the modern credo that we are all free, decisive and rational individuals.

Reason, despite what we would like to think, is not why we do what we do: it is the result of what we feel or do.

Famed adman David Ogilvy recognized this long ago when he wrote:

"Customers need a rational excuse to justify their emotional decisions. So always include one."

(In France I once saw this expressed as "le rationnel est l'alibi du désir".)

Why I love this observation is that Ogilvy uses a word not often given an airing in the communications business: excuse. Not reason or even (eugh) *benefit or proposition*, but excuse.

This is so psychologically on the button that you wonder why we don't have the honesty to admit it more often: the truth is that we are emotionally driven, and more often than not, reasons are only used later by our psychological immune system to deliver some form of justification, be it genuine or not.

Secondly, as a great copywriter, admire the second sentence and its almost dismissively simple tone. Ogilvy is slyly suggesting that the process of having a rational benefit in your advertising should be seen as little more than an "oh, and by the way..."

Brands have belatedly taken on the emotional challenge, especially those which have pinned their brand to the most positive emotion, of happiness. The Coca Cola happiness factory, the Cadbury campaign which started with a "glass and a half of happiness" and has moved on to "welcome to Joyville", or the BMW range with its suspiciously totalitarian: "BMW is joy". Not that this automatically guarantees a brand's success, but an emotional focus has been demonstrated to be a pre-requisite of communications success.

At the other end of the emotional spectrum, disgust has been relatively neglected except, it seems, by charities. In the UK, the RSPCA often evokes this emotion to highlight the plight of abandoned or mistreated animals and the children's charity Barnardo's once got into trouble with the regulatory authorities with images of infants shooting up drugs.

My favourite demonstration was a poster for the charity the British Heart Foundation. It pointed out the link between smoking and heart disease, by showing how smoking can build up fat deposits in the arteries. It showed, very simply a cigarette with a slit through to reveal a tube of fat. (Eugh!).

As psychotherapist Adam Phillips explained: Freud not only showed how irrational we are, but how irrational rationality is.

One of the implications is that, whereas reason leads to calculation and conclusions (only), it is emotion that leads to action because evolution has primed emotions to be its main executioners, which act as overrides in important situations in which rational calculation can waste time and resources.

It also makes life messier in terms of how we measure emotion (rational messages being so much easier to prepare for formulaic and quantitative measurement, which is why the research industry is striving hard to catch up and finds ways of capturing and measuring emotional responses).

The emotional brain is in charge of this rational deck (in the manner of Captain Kirk) but operates more as Mr Spock in a blind refusal to acknowledge the power and passion of emotion. The new model accepts that, when there is a battle between emotion and reason, emotion wins. The whole behavioural economics programme, and especially Kahneman and Tversky's work on cognitive biases, just reinforces how the brain is designed not to think, but to help us survive and reproduce above all: it demands victory not truth.

When it comes to developing communications programmes, this means we must appreciate that engaging emotions and eliciting an emotional response should be the primary task of all communications. This is because creative advertising gets more attention, forms stronger memories and is more likely to be recalled, so simple and consistent messages will create stronger memories. In short, the more creative and emotional an advert is, the better it will work: rather than emotion being a "nice to have", it is essential and a powerful driver of business success. There has been a recent avalanche of evidence from the likes of the Institute of Practitioners in Advertising (IPA), the body that represents advertising agencies and their interests, to prove that emotional campaigns are more effective and profitable, as well as yielding more profitable brands.

Moral: never underestimate the power of emotion. Consider how you are going to be influencing the emotions of your audiences. Specifically:
- What are the emotional start points for your audience?
- What are the key emotions you are expecting to stimulate? Are you making the audience happy? Who might feel sad? Is there anyone in which you might inspire anger? What fears are the audience facing about their market or brand? How do you acknowledge this?
- How would you feel if you received the presentation you're giving?
- Can you make drama out of this by explicitly acknowledging the emotions you will be touching throughout?

TIP 7: GRAB THEM EARLY OR *START TO STARTLE*

Part of the blueprint for successful storytelling is starting with a bang. Grab the attention of your audience early and it will ensure that their interest is piqued. This is all neuroscientifically validated: the brain desires coherence above everything and seeks cognitive ease, according to Daniel Kahneman, which means it finds it easy to follow a prescribed path. This in turn encourages a degree of priming in the audience, who are subtly led in the direction you are seeking to take them in.

Grabbing attention early is a feature of much art.

But the principles remain the same with our communications.

First, there is scene-setting. As with books or films, when we grab our audience early we establish the atmosphere and mood.

Second, in so doing we start setting expectations of what is to come: later, we will talk about the thread that we initiated. By grabbing attention early, we are starting to unwind the thread. As we have said, the brain responds positively to this pattern.

Finally, how we begin our communication inspires curiosity and primes attention. In our goal to secure and hold attention, it is important that we start as we mean to go on and lay down a marker that we intend to resist the siren call of distraction.

Look at these examples of opening lines from literature and see if you can stop yourself from wanting to read on.

[For those umm-ing and ahh-ing, answers in the notes.]

SOME FIRST LINES FROM LITERATURE

1. As Gregor Samsa awoke one morning from uneasy dreams, he found himself transformed into a giant insect.
2. No one would have believed in the last years of the nineteenth that this would be watched keenly and closely by intelligences greater than man's and yet as mortal as his own.
3. If you really want to hear about it, the first thing you'll probably want to know is where I was born, and what my lousey childhood was like, and how my parents were occupied and all before they had me, and all that David Copperfield kind of crap, but I don't feel like going into it, if you want to know the truth.
4. It was a bright cold day in April, and the clocks were striking thirteen.

Karin Fong is a director and designer and is responsible for creating title sequences for film and television including *Boardwalk Empire*, *Terminator: Salvation*, *Charlotte's Web*, and *Rubicon*. She explains how she sees the role of title sequences in telling a story:

"Opening titles are an invitation. Good ones stir feelings of anticipation, making it easy for the viewer to join in. The title sequence becomes a passageway into the show. It says, 'pay attention now – you are leaving your everyday life behind. It's the curtain that rises up, telling you to suspend your disbelief. It's the 'once upon a time' that signifies a story is about unfold."

Writers and theorists suggest that a good opening line can make or break a good novel. Perhaps my favourite opening line comes from the late Iain Banks' 1992 novel, The Crow Road: *"It was the day my grandmother exploded"*. I won't spoil it for you, but this line is brave, surreal and holds you in its palm until you resolve its enigma.

So why not start your presentation like this, where the big idea, the insight, the story starts and primes...

THE TOP DOWN APPROACH

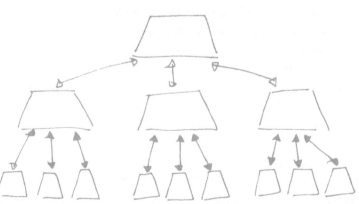

....rather than what tends to happen in many cases: so much introductory waffle which obscures your story and frustrates your audience?

THE NORM?

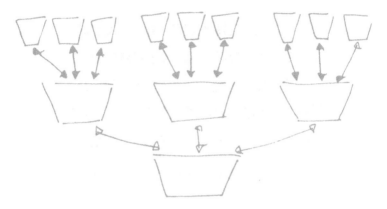

Your opening could be any or all of the following:
- The conclusion upfront
- An unexpected and disorientating insight or recommendation
- An ambiguity, which will leave your audience wanting resolution and the dénouement
- Invitational and embracing: "Come and let me take you on a journey"

There is nothing more compelling than setting our brain a question or puzzle that it cannot help but try to decode, that asks, "I dare you not to read on..."

TIP 8: BUILDING CHARACTER

> "The essence of story is someone overcoming tremendous obstacles (internal or external) to reach a desired goal."
>
> (Richard Krevolin, author and screenwriter)

Different experts on storytelling cite differing requirements for the structure of story and it is self-evident that some aspects of storytelling and narrative will not have an exact correspondence with business communications.

But many of the key components do have a relevance to the art of better communication and presentation.

One of the most basic and effective elements of storytelling, that we all instinctively comprehend, is the idea of character, or personality. It seems that even animals may have personality. We all appreciate a central character or hero in a story; someone for whom we root, with whom we empathize and engage, whose experience we experience.

As you sit in front of your PowerPoint deck, your Word document or spreadsheet you may not naturally be thinking of Odysseus, Moses, Frodo or Harry Potter. But at the risk of stretching the analogy too far until it tweaks a hamstring, I do think there are some ways in which bringing these ideas of storytelling into your communications will bear enlightening fruit [apology for the mixed metaphors].

TIME FOR SOME MORE ETYMOLOGY

There are connections to be discovered between the idea of "character" and the concept of the brand. The word brand, we sometimes forget, comes from the notion of the branding iron, from an era in which it was important to mark and distinguish your cattle from your neighbours' cattle.

Two implications arise from this dip into the history of human-bovine relationships:

The first is that the notion of branding is inextricably linked with the idea of burning something into something else (usually the brand name or some associations into the brains of people, with all the attendant implications of consumer-as-cattle, and of power, control and ownership: ideas that seem unhelpful to say the least).

The second is the proximity of the idea of "brand" to that of "character". The latter word, which we see everywhere, can mean a defining quality or personality; a sense of moral strength; or an individual within a book, play or film, and has the same root. "Character" comes from the word meaning "to engrave" or "inscribe". So when brand theorists, such as (not that...) Stephen King, evoked the idea of "brand personality" in the 1970s, they were on firm historical and linguistic footing, though it was not so much anthropomorphic as bovo-morphic.

As we shall see when we look at conflict, there can be no character without conflict: there should always be a sense of a clash of opposites, a rivalry and collision of different views and behaviours.

Here are five ways in which to explore the notion of building character into your presentations:

- People
- Companies
- Brands
- "Consumer" or consumer groups
- Ideas

a) The most obvious place to start will be with people featured in your presentation. Is there a person at the heart of what you want to say? Someone in your audience, someone whose behaviour you are trying to modify? Why not consider how to build their story into your presentation: their back-story, the tasks ahead, how they responded and how they achieved what they sought to?

b) If addressing someone directly is not considered appropriate, is it feasible to make the *company* or organization you are talking to the hero of your tale? A remarkably large number of books are written about the modern company (mainly "Apple" it seems), and many of these are told as stories of success and failure, redemption, the kingdoms of emperors and visionaries, and their obstacles, trials and quests.

Personalizing a company may also make the imparting of information easier to both create and receive.

c) The third route may come more naturally. As we saw, the word character comes from the Greek for "stamp" and is therefore closely related to the notion of "brand". So, why not think of the brand as your central character?

When we look at the golden thread in the next topic, we will see how building the spine of your presentation around a marketing or business theme will naturally lend it a skeleton that allows the virtues of narrative to shine through rather than constructing sequences of meandering events or numbers.

Think about how the brand can fit into any number of existing story frames:

* Can your storytelling demonstrate how its "arc" has moved over the period you are exploring? Is it a story of success or failure, growth or decline?
* What is your role: chronicler, protagonist, Greek chorus observing and commenting on what the audience sees?
* What is the brand's antagonist? What is their Pepsi to Coca Cola, their PC to Mac? Their Branson to…pretty much anyone. How can you create or dramatize the conflict?

d) If you are in the research or insight business, you may well have a natural protagonist in the form of the "consumer".

There is no substitute for a really good piece of pen portraiture, which goes beneath the mundane stereotypes, demographic banalities and templates of the majority of marketing and research analysis and depiction. Good targeting will always achieve the twin goals of identifying the right audience/s (who are they and the substantiation for choosing them over other groups), and then portraying them in as vivid and enlightening a form as possible.

Below is an example I wrote a while back, looking at young people and their relationship to gum and mints. Note how this is written "outside-in", as people (youths, social animals, and their need to find themselves) first and buyers second, and how unapologetically journalistic it is in style.

Finally to look, once again, outside the traditional halls of the business world, there are some striking instances of popular books that place ideas-as-characters in the foreground.

THE LIFE OF A 17-YEAR-OLD

You're at a crossroads. "When your mentality... catches up with your biology" as the singer songwriter Morrissey once crooned, it is a time of profound uncertainty. The pursuit of a glorious future, career, job satisfaction, independence, idealism, money; and/or the threat of unemployment, sex, relationships, and pragmatic responsibility.

The joyous flight from childhood and adolescence, the quest for all the siren lures of adulthood. The changing of your own personality as it is exposed to all the challenges of the world you've always half craved, half feared.

What keeps you going (or centred, or focused) are your mates: your family or your passions. The pressure from family and media is now more on the boys who, more often than not, lack a 'Map of Life'.

Various accessories and weapons help you navigate the Sea of Uncertainty. Primarily, it's the communal discoveries:

meeting boys/girls together, discussing them, looking for jobs, hanging out, chilling, pubs and clubs.

The mobile, brass in pocket and ciggies are all social lubricants.

Alongside these are the social currency of mints and gum. Their vital role is as a kind of transformer: after all the self-imposed excesses of the mad social maelstrom – strong drinks, spicy food, late nights, more strong drinks – they act as a sort of handy fairy godmother. Had too much peppered salami and cheesy Doritos? Breath like Mr Evans from geography? One too many vodka Red Bulls last night?

Pop one of these and all seems (at any rate) better. You can face that interview, you can meet Claire, you can ask your dad for that £50 for new speakers. And if you've run out of these face-savers, you can always cadge some off Kelly: she owes you.

The psychologist Daniel Kahneman, who we saw earlier, spends much of his bestselling publication *Thinking Fast and Slow* elucidating the theory of System 1 and System 2, which we saw earlier. But he states that he will treat each as characters in a psychodrama, with all the conflict that entails, and he does treat the two systems in a way that creates contrast and clarity for the reader.

Similarly, author and thinker Nassim Nicholas Taleb, who we met earlier, creates two characters or alter egos, Fat Tony and Nero Tulip, to illustrate his views in *The Black Swan* and *Antifragile*.

Best-selling author Malcolm Gladwell was the master of this. In *The Tipping Point* he created what those of us in marketing would recognize as a segmentation: he distinguished "connectors", whose main role was as links or nodal points; "translators" who took edgy ideas and accommodated them for the mainstream (Madonna, for example); and "mavens" whose primary role is as experts, repositories of Aristotle's ethos.

Most recently New York Times writer David Brooks' *The Social Animal* gave his take on the neuroscientific revolution, but rather than the standard journalistic thesis he builds a narrative structure, featuring characters called Erica and Harold

"I use them," Brooks writes, *"to describe how genes shape individual lives, how brain chemistry works in particular cases, how family structure and cultural patterns influence development."*

TIP 9: CREATE CONFLICT OR FICTION THROUGH FACTION

"We're more of the love, blood, and rhetoric school. Well, we can do you blood and love without the rhetoric, and we can do you blood and rhetoric without the love, and we can do you all three concurrent or consecutive. But we can't give you love and rhetoric without the blood. Blood is compulsory."

(Tom Stoppard, playwright, Rosencrantz & Guildenstern Are Dead)

Why is conflict so crucial to storytelling and why does it come so naturally to us?

Well it's back to a bit of neuroscience for an explanation. It seems that our brains are designed with conflict in mind (as it were). The neuroscientist (and novelist) David Eagleman suggests that the brain runs on drama and compares the brain to the famous advisors of President Lincoln: the team of rivals, different neural factions with different causes to fight for and perspectives to defend. Others have used the analogy of Darwinian competition to see the "team of rivals" approach as one of competition between neural networks.

(This is what I refer to in consumer targeting terms as the Many Mes approach: to assume we are the same consistent series of attitudes and behaviours across all moments, moods and markets is a simplistic delusion.)

If you doubt that your brain is constantly in conflict, try the famous marshmallow test. Can you resist having one now if you are promised two tomorrow? Many of these inner conflicts evolve around short-term gratification pitted against longer-term considerations.

It is what has led to the creation of so-called "Ulysses contracts": where we force ourselves to change behaviour by making it impossible. Notice there is nothing here about attitude changing. For example, those with a tendency to max out their credit cards are instructed to put their card in the freezer, and literally freeze their spending. Or, more prosaically, if like me you have an unhealthy fixation on unhealthy confectionery, simply remove it from your home.

In the language of the behavioural economists this equates to the dual process model and the raging tension between System 1 (home of the automatic, implicit and unconscious) and System 2, (the rationalizing, accounting and evaluation system). Much of the conflict (and the reason we systematically under-estimate the power of System 1) is that System 2 feels like the controller, the conscious and decisive "me". This, sadly, appears to be an illusion as it is mostly System 1 which drives our desires to act in accordance with our evolutionary imperatives (survive, thrive, spread genes and develop signalling systems to others).

At one level, conflict is the motor behind the universal human emotion that is surprise. After all, we all know the feeling when awareness of our surroundings occurs only when sensory inputs suddenly violate – or conflict with – our expectations.

So, think of conflict as a major component of your storytelling.

Some examples of how to look for the conflict at the heart of your presentation might include:
1. Is the conflict between what you were asked to investigate and what you have found?
2. Is it between members of your audience? Often there will be contradictory expectations and political positions espoused by your audience, or by members of your organization, which you are addressing explicitly.
3. Often the greatest conflict is between what your audience is expecting and what you are delivering. Make the most of this conflict. Signal it early and drive it home.

4. You many find that you are creating a conflict between what you were asked to look at ("the brief") and what you have found (in your research, analysis).
5. How can you most expressively highlight the conflict (differences) between this "consumer" and others that you have identified but rejected?
6. How does this target differ from what the previous identification or depiction was?
7. How does this affect your brand and comms targeting? What may need changing?
8. Might there be inherent conflict within the company, between different divisions or even (perish the thought) between client and agency?

TIP 10: STAY JUNG; USE ARCHETYPES

It's not just in the domain of brands and marketing that we find symbols have such an influence over us.

A symbol is an image or thing that acquires its symbolic value through the meanings and emotions it evokes in us, and semiotics is becoming an increasingly potent way of understanding how brands can affect us.

Here, I want to look at one class of symbols, what are known (after Carl Jung) as archetypes. Archetypes provide a bridge between the conscious and the unconscious, and especially the twilight zone that Jung called "the collective unconscious".

Ethnographers and anthropologists have discovered that there are certain basic characters (or types) that occur in ancient myths or fairytales and also in stories, literature and film. The Austrian psychoanalyst and colleague of Jung, Otto Rank, claimed that "myth is the collective dream of the people".

Freud and Jung, of course, did much to demonstrate the centrality of primordial stories from fairytales, mythology and religion across time and cultures. Jung's emphasis on the role of archetypes is still at work in how we (in the media and marketing) collectively stereotype groups based on preconceived *idées reçues* (or, sometimes, *idées fixes*). Acknowledging the influence of Plato's forms, Jung believed that archetypes provide a tapestry of language and help create the collective unconscious.

We are in many ways "homo symbolicus" using archetypes to help us navigate the world of symbols and meanings. Because these archetypes relate to our deepest, most emotional universal desires they are incredibly powerful as deep themes that can engage attention.

Change and transformation is not limited, of course, to Greek and Roman myth. Journalist and author Christopher Booker, in his account of the common plots and archetypes across humanity's stories, argues that all the basic plots found in storytelling are about personal transformation.

Most transformations centre on quests: think of Hercules's labours; Aeneas' return to Troy; Theseus taking on the Minotaur (see Tip 11, opposite); Odysseus's challenge-strewn journey home to his wife Penelope in Ithaca; the search for the Holy Grail; Dorothy's mission in The Wizard of Oz; and Luke Skywalker's quest to find his true history.

So consider identifying the quest in your story by answering these questions:
1. What is the 'inner quest'?
2. What is the transformation?
3. Who is or are the heroes?
4. What is your tone or personality?

TIP 11: **THE GOLDEN THREAD**

The benefits of a classical education are manifold: erudition, eloquence and the ability to use words like desuetude or litotes in public without fear or shame, not to mention the chance of being elected Mayor of London.

But it brings with it too a raft of gorgeously enriching stories and revealing metaphors. So far, we have referred to the myth of Dionysus and Pentheus representing passion and logic, to the wanderings of Odysseus, and talked about various archetypal quest stories.

Now we move on to the story of Theseus and Ariadne, which is both striking and under-appreciated (unless you are a Jungian psycho-analyst).

According to the orthodox version of the legend, King Minos of Crete demanded that the Athenians send seven young men and seven young women every nine years – other accounts say every year – to be sacrificed to his offspring, the Minotaur, the creature that was half-man and half-bull.

(Fans of *The Hunger Games* may appreciate that author Suzanne Collins has acknowledged the debt owed to the Minotaur myth in her series.)

One year, the sacrificial party included Theseus, a young man who volunteered to come and kill the Minotaur. Minos's daughter Ariadne fell in love with Theseus, and helped him by giving him a ball of golden thread, so that once he had slain the Minotaur he could find his way safely out of the Minotaur's labyrinth.

The story of the golden thread can give us a clue as to how to guide ourselves out of the labyrinth of disconnected data and chaos within which, in the business world, we too often find ourselves mired.

Talking of etymology, the word "clue" is itself derived from the Anglo-Saxon word "clew", or ball of thread. Greek mythology was rich in fabric symbolism, the three Fates being Clotho (the spinner: and seemingly not etymologically related to "cloth") who prepares the thread of life, Lachesis (the allotter), who measures it out, and Atropos (unturnable or inevitable) who cuts it off. Hindu literature shares the same interest in cloth: the sutra (best known in the west when preceded by Kama) was the thread that held things together. Similarly, tantra [again the main link is with things erotic and Sting] comes from the concept of the loom or warp.

I don't want to pursue the symbolic or Jungian aspects of the story, but I want to use the idea of the golden thread as a metaphor for describing the issue of editing and constructing in a way that makes story central to how we present and communicate in the work environment.

THE STRICTURE OF STRUCTURE

"Structure is the most important thing of all, I think, in writing. You may think of a marvellous plot, but unless you know how to structure it, which bit goes where and where, you won't get the full impact of it." (Beryl Bainbridge, novelist).

Substance is nothing without structure. Content is nothing without form. The most important element of a picture is the frame, as the essence of all art is limitation and stricture.

This is why the communications industry has creative briefs and why narrative is the glue without which your presentation quickly falls apart.

Yet too often the material we present lacks anything so much as a pattern or structure, let alone a story. As we have seen, the brain craves pattern and order, yet structure is so often missing in action.

The golden thread is really my way of insisting on the importance of editing, tightness and framing. It is the skeleton, the foundation for the thinking and the journey that you are taking your audience on. And the first rule of any journey is that nobody likes getting lost, marooned or abandoned.

All storytellers insist that the most essential principle of telling a story is what to include and what to leave out [this should remind us of the principle of 'exformation']. In business, we are generally not very adept at listening to this advice, believing that a "full account" should always be given.

Here are a few principles that elaborate the concept of the golden thread.

Shape, structure and edit:

As we saw earlier, information carries within it the kernel of "form" and shape. Just as the artist chooses exactly what to put inside the frame and therefore, crucially, what to leave *outside* the frame and omit, so should we think harder about what we need to include before we automatically put everything in "to be safe".

So, start by finding the golden thread.

- What is the argument you are making?
- What is the question you are answering?
- Or what is the new question you are posing?
- What is the business issue about which you are delivering a point of view?
- What is the insight you have uncovered?
- What is the platform you wish to debate and air with the assembled attendees?
- What is the *meaning* that will affect your audience, their worries and/or the "consumer"?

Once you have worried your way through the data, or the material you have, take the time to identify your golden thread. If it helps, consult colleagues (if you are doing a team presentation, such as a pitch, this will be inevitable).

Let the argument lead you, especially if there is a lack of consensus.

I have found, when working on presentations, that more than one golden thread may be available. In this case, you can either:

- Agree on the one that you think represents the best fit, and adapt the rest of your material to make sure that it becomes subsumed under the one golden thread
- Or prepare the material so that you present alternative scenarios or hypotheses but ensure that from the start you have signposted the fact that you will have more than one thread (what if you relaunch the brand as a premium offering? What if you create a new brand to target non-users solely? What if you scrap it entirely?)

One way of thinking about structure is like metre in poetry or genre in popular culture (such as movies). Both create the frame, the sense of category conventions and expectations, which can then be followed or subverted.

TIP 12: SOME DATA-DAY HELP

Now something for those whose day-to-day lives involve data days.

When searching for the golden thread and for a more systematic and purposeful way of moving from data to meaning, I always ask which of the two following models people feel happiest with:
- Data as directive
- Data as confirmation

If you feel naturally inclined to let the data direct you without assuming any prior hypotheses, you may subscribe to the view that the purity of the data is all. As you may have already guessed, I am not of this view, being a fully-paid-up post-modernist who believes that "truth" – outside of science – is, by and large, socially constructed.

But because many of the people I have trained and many of you reading this now are likely to be data users, whether qualitative or quantitative data, I will outline the pros and cons of each approach.

DATA AS DIRECTIVE
The attraction of letting the data direct you is that it encourages you to be as thorough as required. It allows you to be systematic and logical in the way you deal with the data; "objective", even, if you feel comfortable with that as a *modus operandi*. This is the more classic, textbook way of approaching data that many in the market research industry have been trained to adopt as second nature.

The sense of immersion can be very refreshing, bathing naked in streams of data.

The potential limitation of this method is that it inevitably takes time: I mention this not to suggest that you skimp on the data gathering and analysis, but to point out that much of what I am proposing here about storytelling is sometimes criticized for "taking up time that I don't have". My rebuttal would be that it can accelerate the speed at which data is processed by the brain, thereby not only making your output more insightfully effective but actually saving time in the long-run.

This links to my next point. Sometimes, the problem associated with wilfully clearing your mind of hypotheses and ideas is – apologies for arboreal cliché – that you "cannot see the wood for the trees". The data branches out in so many directions that the brain struggles to impose focus, loses control and yearns for "cognitive ease".

DATA AS CONFIRMATION

On the other hand, if you go into a data-bath armed with a hypothesis or several, and a sponge, the advantage is that it allows you to look into and through the material at a much faster pace. The brain, as we saw, works more smoothly when it is running on heuristic paths: hypotheses can be elegant ways of seeing patterns in the data in a more focused fashion, because we feel more involved and engaged with the process, rather than the more awkward approach of deliberately disengaging our evolved tendency to look for new patterns and verify existing ones. As we noted earlier, the pattern-tate brain will naturally seek out frames, ideas and regularities, so having pre-prepared frameworks is likely to speed up the whole process. This, in turn, generates more "big picture ideas", more wood than trees.

This is the approach I favour, personally, though I appreciate, from long years of working at the coalface and in training, that many feel instinctively uncomfortable with this. So, for those who do, and for the rest of us who need to be aware of the risks, here are a few things of which to be aware when using what is sometimes called the hypothetico-deductive model.

- First of all, it is essential to make oneself aware of the risk attached to early fixity (in medical language, this is called premature anticipation). I don't want to point the finger at the brain (again), but....
- Confirmation bias means that once it has lighted upon something it likes, the brain will naturally go out of its way to seek out only evidence that supports that idea. This bias is something that we have to be aware of as we develop our thinking and golden thread in case we have become too committed to an outcome without considering evidence that might disprove it. So I would counsel that we ensure we feel happy that we have come to terms with all the data (or as much as we think we can realistically) before finally making that commitment.

Can I offer a compromise? What I find really helpful, as a "confirmed confirmer", is making a conscious decision to postulate as *many competing hypotheses* upfront as I can. This has several advantages.

First, it means your brain cannot lazily and automatically default to the one favoured hypothesis that it finds most convenient, because there is more than one to contend with.

Second, it means that you (your brain, whoever) can actively search out parallel and competing data, which can also assuage your guilt that you are not doing justice to the whole dataset.

Finally, it means you can deliver alternative golden threads, which may be exactly what is required. So for a pitch, rather than just arbitrarily arguing for one creative route or strategy, you can play the "we looked at routes A, B and C, but discounted them for the following reasons and went with this idea for the following reasons". In a research debrief, you can follow a similar path and argue that the product, brand or marketing solution that best cleaves to the data is Route X.

TWO APPROACHES

DATA AS DIRECTIVE		DATA AS CONFIRMATION	
+	**–**	**+**	**–**
Thorough	Takes time	Fast-moving	Too early fixity
Logical	More Trees than Wood	Involving	Too committed
"textbook" way		Framework	Not coming to terms with all info
...for those who wish to immerse	Can lead to lack of focus	More Wood than Trees	

TIP 13: WRITE LESS THINK MORE

One of the *"T-shirt-able principles"* I would like you to take away [and ideally turn into a T-shirt-ready slogan] is *"to write less and think more"*.

As we saw in Part 2, the principle of exformation, the culling of what obstructs the simplicity and directness of a message, is still under-appreciated in the world of business communications. How many times have you asked for more charts? How often do you feel that you are on the receiving end of (or even perpetrating) "one damn thing after another?" This is like the joke about people having on their tombstone:

A STORY OF RELENTLESS REITERATION

I was speaking at a conference a couple of years ago and on the bill was a speaker representing a well-known advertising medium. I like this medium and happen to think that there are loads of great examples of how to use it creatively and effectively. The speaker also believed this. However, he chose to make this point by reiterating it relentlessly (irritating alliteration intended). He showed a great ad. Then another. Then another. And another. Then, guess what, another. After about 10 examples and 15 minutes, the audience had switched off and begun to ponder how many consonants there were in Mississippi.

Why? Because there was no argument, no thread to follow that gave our pattern-tate brain a hook to cling to, a pattern to seek out.

"I wish I'd spent more time in the office".

This simple truth is so often neglected, even (especially?) among so-called creatives.

Recall how often you have really wished, with all your heart, with hands clasped together in a Disneyesque pose, that the interminable chart dumpage to which you were being subjected during a presentation could be halted immediately.

There are countless ways now to ensure that minutiae and bottoms are covered (I'm thinking of a demanding research manager here who needs a record of where the depth interviews were carried out, or the sample sizes for relevant sub-groups who had seen the ad but hadn't used the brand).

We will come back to this later, but having more than one deck for different needs and audiences is one fairly straightforward response.

So this becomes as much a matter of *focus* as time. But it is essential to try to avoid getting buried in the detail and spend time reducing, simplifying and structuring. The returns on thinking far outweigh the "extra" time.

Nobody will appreciate your ideas being buried underneath a "data duvet", the appealingly soft and comforting layers of data, information and verbiage.

Like other addictive substances, they tend to be used to disguise or assuage underlying problems instead of treating fundamental concerns that created them.

Ask yourself: how much can you (safely) remove? How much can you relocate to an appendix, to the Q&As at the end of the session or any subsequent meeting?

Let's again look to the celebrated screenwriter, David Mamet:
"How much can one remove and still have the composition be intelligible? This understanding, or its lack, divides those who can write from those who can really write. Chekhov removed the plot. Pinter, elaborating, removed the history, the narration; Beckett, the characterization. We hear it anyway. Omission is a form of creation."

The thinking can be done in isolation, with just you, your quill pen and a blank papyrus; or collectively, where you can bounce your hypotheses off colleagues, who (ideally) are not part of the same project or presentation, thus making them outsiders. But, you may object, we can make things too short, too simple? Don't we risk throwing out the baby (of meaning) with the murky bathwater (of data)?

I repeat: "Have you ever thought you needed more charts to make a point?" As we saw before, the more information we are given, the more the brain is likely to challenge it. In a series of experiments carried out at Carnegie Mellon University, students were given 20-30 minutes with two sets of information across a range of subjects. One was a full chapter of 5,000 words, the other a summary of 1,000 words. The students were tested both 20 minutes after reading the material, and again a year later. In both cases they learned more from the summaries than they did from the whole chapter.

Another classic experiment carried out by Paul Slovic, professor of psychology at Oregon University, looked at the ability of eight handicappers to predict the outcome of horse races. He tested different levels: first, the handicappers could use any five pieces of information they wanted; then he increased it, incrementally, to 10 pieces of information, 20, and finally, 40. He was examining how stress is caused by information overload. When the handicappers' predictions were analyzed against the actual outcomes of the 40 races, it became clear that the increase in levels on information made no difference to their overall level of predictive accuracy. All that did change was their degree of reported confidence.

TIP 14: THE BEGINNING, MIDDLE AND THE END...

"A story should have a beginning, middle and end but not necessarily in that order."

(French film director and theorist Jean-Luc Godard)

Everything we have said about grabbing attention early should make it clear that an effective headline and a positive start is crucial in order to attract the reader/listener/viewer and provide a taste of what is to come.

Writers always advise that the first 10 pages of a script should be the best. If your audience doesn't want to read on (or continue to listen/watch) you have failed.

A good headline – with a clear golden thread – will ensure that whoever is listening, watching or reading you will be primed to know where they are going, what to look for and will not feel lost, bemused or frustrated.

Just as genre plays with structure, so we should consider how to escape the prison of predictability.

A STORY: THE PITCH

To take an example from the marketing world: the pitch presentation.

Too often I have observed, or even been party to, a presentation to a client for their business. The session – let us assume it is 60 minutes, maybe 90 if the client is only seeing 10 to 12 agencies – proceeds as follows:

- How lovely the audience/client is and how humble and honoured the agency feels to pitch for its beauteous and bounteous business.
  - Five minutes on the rehearsal time-sheet, 10 minutes in practice. Audience putting on "politely indulgent but anxious" faces.
- This is our agency; gaze at and admire how wonderful and handsome/sexy we all are and in how many parts of the globe we are represented.
  - One minute in rehearsal, 10 minutes if the CEO is on a roll of blistering self-adoration. Clients visibly shifting, looking at each other.
- This is the brief you so generously and adorably gave us (and that you therefore know more intimately than we do, given that you spent months writing the thing, and have heard, or will hear, five to 10 other competing, and broadly similar, agencies reiterate it in similar fashion).
  - Five to 10 more minutes of insightlessness. CEO thinking of what time he needs to wake up to get to Heathrow by 7.30 am.

- Appreciate the lovingly conducted background research and sumptuous fact-finding that we did, just for you. (And that all the other agencies did too, with a corresponding level of veneration, so nothing new there.)
- Five minutes, 10 to 15 if the planner is unleashed. Attendees are now worrying that the planner is one chart away from imploding, and are giving unnecessary headspace to anticipating the arrival of biscuits; they are hoping these are more thickly chocolate-coated than the previous agency's.
- The "what we found about your market/brand" section. Have they actually started now? Yes, but this is predominantly material that we know (if only because we gave you the documents you are synthesising in only slightly less detail than the originals).
- 10 minutes, 15 if the planner starts using typically recherché terms. (Audience reaction: "When's lunch?")
- And then......

You get the point. It may well be that half the allotted time has passed before the attendees have heard anything new, interesting or sufficiently distracting to pull them out of their confectionery-directed reverie. If they are coming expressly to hear something that will reframe their brand, galvanize the trade, impress Geneva or re-energize the "consumer", be it an insight or a piece of creative magic, why put all these obstacles in the way?

This is because the genre conventions become so entrenched that the audience's expectations are swept aside in an orgy of self-congratulation.

Hear Me! Adore me! Follow my counsel, for I am wise and internally-revered beyond knowing!

So, for a pitch or sales presentation why not:

1. Start with the story, the insight, the moment of truth, the end, not the beginning. Begin with a headline or argument that will immediately grab attention, and make attendees anticipate (and salivate for) what is to come. Don't just use banal business terms that bleed the interest out of everyone.

2. Prioritize the audience's key concern, worry (or "pain" to use the current term du jour). Why not start by acknowledging it and maybe even answer it upfront, before explaining your working out?

3. Relegate the "who we are and how wonderful" stuff to the document, the website, to the Q&As. Do not apologize for doing this.

4. Simplify and hunt down exformation.

   - When I work with agencies or clients on presentations, the single biggest area I work on is reducing, simplifying and structuring.
   - Does that chart really need to be there? Why is that graph there? Remember the Latin expression "cui bono?" (whom does it benefit?).
   - The answer in this case is usually the person who wrote it, often to justify their part in proceedings, or the Deliverer collectively rather than the ultimate Receiver. Leave the ego aside, and cut it.

5. Be coherent: part of the problem with the story above is that it lacks coherence. It is one section after the other, and has no thread other than "how wonderful we are...here we are being wonderful for you". Start upfront with the structure you are going to be following (and no, not just introduction, background fact-finding, the consumer).

TIP 15: BE THREE THINKING

Like ethos, logos and pathos and so many other unwitting examples in this book, the division into three seems to be exceptionally common. Beginning, middle and end being the most obvious.

The forefathers of rhetorical thinking, Cicero and Quintilian, divided up the theory of oratory into five parts: invention, arrangement, style, memory and delivery.

Breaking this down further, the author of the *Ad Herennium* (often thought to be Cicero) segments the second part, arrangement, into five sections. In discussing two of these sections – narration and division – the author states:

"The Distribution has two parts: the Enumeration and the Exposition. We shall be using the Enumeration when we tell by number how many points we are going to discuss. The number ought not to exceed three; for otherwise, besides the danger that we may at some time include in the speech more or fewer points than we enumerated, it instils in the hearer the suspicion of premeditation and artifice, and this robs the speech of conviction."

It has often been said that "three is a magic number", not least at the launch of the BBC TV channel of that number. But the number three does seem to have some deep-seated and universal force. One is absolute, two is for comparison and contrast and three seems to be a convenient blend of cumulative force without testing memory or patience.

Rhetoric has a special term for this (as it does for most human expressions): the *tricolon*.

They are surprisingly ubiquitous from classical speeches, to modern politicians to the ad industry.

- *"Veni, vidi, vici"* ("I came, I saw, I conquered", which was said by Julius Caesar, who also bequeathed to generations of soon-to-be-tricolonic Latin students the memorable "Gaul as a whole is divided into three parts")
- "Blood, sweat and tears" (Winston Churchill)
- *"Liberté, Égalité, Fraternité"* (the French motto)
- *The Good, The Bad and The Ugly* (film directed by Sergio Leone)
- *Sex, Lies and Videotape* (laurel-winning Steven Soderbergh film, much spoofed on, and after, release)
- Peter Greenaway's *The Cook, The Thief, His Wife and Her Lover* broke the mould and also became the source of much parody and repetition.
- "I think we've all arrived at a very special place. Spiritually, ecumenically, grammatically." (Captain Jack Sparrow in the film *Pirates of the Caribbean: Curse of the Black Pearl*)
- *Quark, Strangeness and Charm* (album by Hawkwind)
- "Citius, altius, fortius" (faster, higher, stronger); the Olympic motto and all the more powerful in the Latin.
- "Wine, women and song" (source uncertain, and probably rejected early on in the process of choosing the Olympic motto).
- "I require three things in a man. He must be handsome, ruthless, and stupid." (Dorothy Parker)

- "Eye it, try it, buy it" (classic slogan for Chevrolet; in the UK, retailer Argos's "Find It. Get it. Argos it" strives for the same cumulative power and simplicity.)
- "Thinner, faster, lighter" (claim made for Apple's iPhone 5)

The comedian's toolbox also includes the rule of three. Comedian and writer Richard Herring acknowledges that there is something satisfying about grouping items in three.

In comedy, the sequence tends to be:

1. Introduce the idea, subject or context
2. Reinforce and emphasize it
3. Contradict or subvert it

This is not a bad rule to follow in arranging and editing your presentation.

1. Three points per slide should be the rule. It will be easier for your brain to process, to use as a prompt, and easier for your audience to understand and recall, especially for live performance.
2. Three should be the basis for the skeleton, the golden thread and the structure of your deck. A beginning middle and end, and each chapter outlined and illustrated by the rule of three. Consider making the three points explicit at the beginning and end of your presentation to reinforce their importance, relevance and significance.
3. Three can be used to build the cumulative force of your argument. Too often, points on charts or in speeches are given no special rhythm, speed or cadence. I would recommend examining some of the above examples to see how they gain in power and momentum and then applying this to your argument.

TIP 16: WRITE, WRITE AND WRITE AGAIN

Novelist EM Forster said something very insightful about the relationship between writing and thinking: "How can I tell what I think until I see what I say?".

The truth behind this aperçu is that it is only in the process of writing and talking that we can genuinely uncover what we feel, believe or think.

So, when we are analyzing data or preparing an argument, the golden thread may (probably will) only emerge in the process of collecting the material, sifting it and (following the theory of what I call insightment) allowing incubation to forge previously unseen links.

In order to make the process of generating insights more fruitful, but also to reduce and simplify, keep writing and keep editing. Every edit will bring new ideas to prominence as the incubatory brain uncovers new connections and insights, and every version will be sharper, simpler and more focused. It only takes one moment, one flash for an insight to appear, and then everything else must be refashioned in its wake.

Screenwriter Charlie Kaufman expressed this nicely in his 2011 speech at the British Academy of Film and Theatre

Awards (BAFTA), where he also reminded us that entertainment is the fundamental level of all forms of storytelling.

"The other thing that happens is adjustment. You find out which part of the story works, which part to embellish, which to jettison. You fashion it. Your goal is to be entertaining. This is true for a story told at a dinner party, and it's true for stories told through movies."

(For someone who wrote a screenplay called Adaptation you would expect him to be a proponent of adjustment.)

Another film writer, Jean-Claude Carrière, whose career stretches from working with Luis Bunuel to Cyrano de Bergerac as well as writing with Umberto Eco, discussed screen writing using this aquatic reference:

"We gather in a circle and I ask one or two of them to give us the very beginning of a story: a desire and an obstacle to that desire. I call them waves: there's a wave of exploration: you open yourself up and let everything come in, and then there's another wave where you go back and see what's left on the sand by the ocean."

The writer Theodore Geisel, better known by his nom de plume, Dr Seuss, was equally insistent about the need to be studiously methodical and prolific.

"For a 60-page book, I may easily write more than 1,000 pages before I'm satisfied. The most important thing about me I feel is that I work like hell --write, re-write, reject, re-reject and polish incessantly."

Cezanne was said to have tried painting his patron Vollard 150 times at one sitting: "Does an apple move?", he inquired impatiently. Mark Twain spent so long revising Huckleberry Finn it took nearly a decade to complete.

More recently, the story of Richard Curtis's screenplay for *Four Weddings and a Funeral* is testament to this polishing and re-polishing. Legend has it that it took 14 re-writes before it got to a version with which everyone, Curtis included, was happy.

TIP 17: SOMETHING FOR THE PEAK END

How can we make our work lives and our clients happier? How can we enhance the sum of happiness of presentations both for those who give them and those who experience them?

Within the wealth of books on the subject of happiness, one element that has been given less recognition, in terms of commercial applicability, than it deserves is the "peak-end rule".

Originally identified by Kahneman, this rule describes the fact that when we recall experienced pleasures it seems to be determined on the basis of two snapshot moments: how any experience felt at its peak (whether good or bad), and how it felt at the *end*.

Much of the original research involved colonoscopy, so as you may just have eaten I will not go into detail here. But other experiments involved examining pleasurable experiences. In one, people were asked to compare holidays. Those who had a shorter vacation that ended spectacularly enjoyed it more than those who had a three-week holiday that also had some great times but ended rather less dramatically.

This indicates that experiences that have clear highs or "spikes" and that end "with a bang" are more likely to be remembered (and remembered fondly) than longer experiences with a more consistent level of intensity.

Think of how endings affect us in sport.

Two personal stories: as a tennis player, I often ponder on how a great point is irrelevant, if my last shot has gone out. Who cares about, or remembers, the stunning return of serve, the fantastic interception I made at the net, followed by the attempted drop shot if my opponent has put the ball away to win the point?

LOVE, DRAMA AND MANCHESTER UNITED

Or take my love of Manchester United football team. As a north Londoner straddling the divide between Arsenal and Spurs, this may need some explanation. I do have family in Manchester.... But there is a special quality about following the team, which makes for drama: its habit of doggedly persevering to the final whistle and scoring late and decisive goals.

Manchester United's recently-retired manager Sir Alex Ferguson, claimed after one game where United snuck in two goals in the last 10 minutes, that this was typical of their style and history. Perhaps the most famous example/s came in the final of the 1999 Champions League, when they were 1-0 down to Bayern Munich in injury time but goals from Ole Gunnar Solskjaer and Teddy Sheringham won it on 90:36 and 92:17 minutes. Now who (apart from Bayern and envious Chelsea, Arsenal and Manchester City fans) remembers the fact that United had been pretty poor for the previous 90 minutes?

Following Man Utd is not just about glory and excellence: it's the love of conflict, surprise, drama and not a little relief.

Many columns and blogs are devoted to the issue of endings: it is a common lament that many great books that we are enjoying at the time leave us without an emotionally satisfying ending, one that makes us feel that we are sated or might even want more. We have all felt that, no matter how brilliant a read it was, it was let down by its ending. [Yes, I am aware of this as I write..]

Let's think of movies again (if you insist). Many have commented on how they loved *Schindler's List*, but found the ending rather mawkish. Some directors have made a career about delivering epic endings (remember M. Night Shyamalan with *The Sixth Sense* or *The Village*).

(Now, reader, significant spoiler alert. The less cine-literate may want to leave, get some popcorn and return in two paragraphs' time.)

Some of my own favourites include the revelation at the end of Adrian Lyne's *Jacob's Ladder*, the "so he's Keyser Soze" moment that concludes *The Usual Suspects*, the "it was all a dream" ending of *The Wizard of Oz*, the "rosebud" revelation in *Citizen Kane*, or the shock twist that ends *Carrie*. *Boogie Nights* offers a rather different type of climax.

Many use great musical pieces to reinforce the crescendo, such as Fight Club (to the tune of The Pixies' *Where is My Mind?*), *Casablanca* and *Dr Strangelove*; some have great lines (how about "nobody's perfect" from *Some Like it Hot*, Anthony Hopkins delivering "I'm having an old friend for dinner" in *The Silence of the Lambs* or Charlton Heston's primal scream at his discovery in *Planet of The Apes: "You did it. You maniacs. You blew it up. Damn you all. G-d damn you all to hell."*)

All of which were not only climactic and striking at the time, but (and I'm guessing your response here) have also taken a comfy seat in your long-term memory.

The screenwriting doyen, Robert McKee puts it like this:
"If you fail to make the poetic leap to a brilliant culminating climax, all previous scenes, characters, dialogue, and description become an elaborate typing exercise."

How this relates to presentations (and all forms of meeting, in fact) should be readily apparent, but is rarely implemented if it is. Not only do most of our decks lack "peak" moments, because they are chart-after-chart of consistent anhedonic mediocrity, but the ending tends to be one of two things.

Either the ending is just a stop, a halt, a freeze-frame or a termination ("you have reached your final destination: please exit the presentation using the stairs to your left by pressing 'escape'"); or the conclusion feels (to use the discredited military metaphor from Part 1), like a ceasefire in the War of Words.

But either way, the main sensation is one of grateful relief.

Instead, think of a pinnacle, a culmination of all the pent-up meaning and emotion towards which you have been building.

The other option is that you have ended your selling sermon with something called "conclusions" (after all it does mean "to close" or "to end", you say). But this is often just a listless list of stuff that you have covered already, and are merely repeating because you feel somehow obliged to repeat it.

So what should we do instead?

The French term "dénouement" is an eloquent word for expressing the meaning of an end. Coming from the root meaning "un-knotting" it reminds us that an ending should be more than just an ending, but a resolution of a conflict, an emotional climax, a satisfying solving of a problem, an unravelling of knots (or threads?) that have been deliberately tied by the author.

(The word climax is from the Greek for ladder: why not write out your ladder? See later under Tip 22, "Storyboard").

Why not consider how to end on a high (note)? As part of your golden thread, ensure that the end is emphatic, dramatic and burns itself onto the synapses of your audience.
* Here is the time to use expressive eloquent language, to reframe and tell the story in its most dramatic and relevant form
* Aim to leave them wanting more, not less

Let the golden thread dictate this, so that everything feels like it has been working towards your climax.

If you achieve this, you may recreate the feeling that Alan Bennett writes of in his play, *The History Boys:*

"You are reading a book and you come across something familiar. It is a thought or an emotion you yourself have had but thought secret, even shameful, peculiar to you. And here it is set down in the book. And it is as if a hand has come out and taken yours."

TIP 18: **THREADING YOUR HYPOTHESIS**

One of the great advantages of being conscious beings is that we can imagine a future. We alone have the ability to conjure up hypotheses, to build models of the future for ourselves or the world, and to recalibrate our thoughts and actions on that speculation. To let our hypotheses die in our stead, as Karl Popper put it, is one of our species' defining characteristics.

This is a form of cognitive play, the sort of playfulness that is essential to creativity.

Stories play a role (as it were) in this, one which perhaps has evolutionary origins and adaptive advantages. Namely, they can act as rehearsals for life and prepare us to explore possibility as much as reality, enhancing our capacity to predict, interpret and respond to events.

SOME CLASSICAL WHAT–IFS
Classical literature is full of the what-ifs and what-nexts of the Homeric stories and, recently, this shows signs of revival. Recently, there has been an outpouring of such Homeric re-imaginings and fillings-out, such as David Malouf's novel

The Ransom, based on book 24 of the Iliad; Zachary Mason's extraordinary *The Lost Books of the Odyssey*, in which he devised dozens of hypothetical narratives for the wandering Odysseus; and Madeline Miller's *Song of Achilles* featuring the boyhoods of Patroclus and Achilles. Other examples of what is known in fiction as "counter-factual history" include Robert Harris's *Fatherland* and Philip Roth's *Plot Against America*.

Speculative fiction could well be a way for us to explore hypotheses about social interaction in a safe way, to train us to explore possibility as well as reality.

This sort of "playful pretence" is also claimed by games-makers, who argue that many of the best video games are microcosms, alternative realities which allow us to indulge our impulse to explore.

As we saw earlier, hypothesis-making is the heart of the scientific enterprise as much as it is in the creative domain. In the research and insight world in which I often dwell, hypothesis is still under-used.

We saw before that finding a golden thread can be assisted in different ways. One of the easiest I find is to consider the thread (or multiple threads) as being derived from business or marketing hypotheses.

1. What business or market are we in? What should we be in? What could we be in?
2. What have you brought to the understanding of the status of the brand and its place in the campaign planning cycle, especially in terms of strategic objectives: where could the brand be,

and how realistic is this? What are the business opportunities? How ambitious are they?

3. In other words, this means framing your golden thread (or threads) in terms of existing or potential marketing hypotheses, for example: If this group of people who currently think this about the brand were instead to think that (or were to think this more intensely), then they would use it more often and sales would increase.

- If the brand were to change in this way or address *this* group instead of *that* the business implications would be *such-and-such.*
- What if the business were to rationalize half its brands globally and invest more heavily in brand building for the remaining three mega-brands?
- What if we quit the market we always thought we were in and instead decided to decamp into the business that consumers seem to think we are in?
- Another way of arranging your thread is not just by making the hypothesis your thread, but your *insight*, something that you know will create surprise and reframe the expectations of your audience.

TIP 19: TWO DECKS GOOD...

Now a warning against thinking of conflating two different presentations into one.

One of my many deeply held philosophical values is that nothing good comes of forcefully blending two disparate components. To advance this philosophical position I offer:

* Jedward (nés John and Edward Grimes), the unfeasibly irritating identical twin singing duo from *The X Factor* who seem to have built a "celebrity" career nonetheless.
* The lazy journalistic habit of creating couples such as Brangelina or, politically/economically Merkozy, the hybrid former leader of France and Germany (or Frarmany). It is a shame that Sarcozy never overlapped with head of former Yugoslavia, Marshall Tito as I would have warmed to a Ti-Cozy.
* Turducken: a US speciality, so I'm told. A chicken stuffed into a duck stuffed inside a turkey. My introduction to this delicacy was actually through cooking programme, *Ace of Cakes*, where they built a turducken cake (no, me neither).
* Beyond poultry, animal breeding is rife with blends. You can choose from a Labradoodle (a Labrador crossed with a poodle) or a Retroodle (retriever and poodle). I am personally trying to breed a Retro-Labradoodle: a Labrador/poodle cross that stays at home watching classic movies.

- As a car advertising veteran, I recall a Nissan Micra campaign which wondered "do you speak Micra?". Before we could answer, it offered some choice coinages such as "spafe" (spacious and safe), "simpology" (simple plus technology). And this without mentioning the others that failed to make a lasting dent in the Oxford English dictionary such as "thractical", "aggrendly", "compacious", "modtro" or "luxurable". Advertising trade magazine, *Campaign*, deftly described it at the time as "shollocks".
- Jeggings: jeans that look like leggings. Or the other way round. They look better than they sound.
- This is all part of the tendency (especially in advertising) to create what I call NOBA (Not Only But Also) brands or messages brilliantly spoofed by legendary US TV show *Saturday Night Live* as far back as 1976 in the *New Shimmer* sketch: "It's a floor wax AND a dessert topping".

Why this natural aversion to blends? Because a blend cannot help but feel like a compromise.

So: Deck 1 is the material we use to present with. Deck 2 is what is to be left as a record of that event.

If necessity is the mother of invention, convenience is the father of compromise, so we create one answer to two different sets of problems: the lowest of common denominators fails on both counts.

Let's just unpack those differing needs for a moment.

DECK 1

Let us call Deck 1 the "presentation deck". This has to communicate the findings, the insights and the point of view as we have been arguing throughout. But because it is presented it is effectively performed, which means that – like it or not – it will inevitably be viewed as in some ways a performance. This means that theatrical conventions will apply: not that you will be judged as though at the Royal Shakespeare Company in Stratford, but nevertheless storytelling and drama will play a part.

Most significantly, it means that you have an audience. A live group of people hanging on your every word and gesture, and the moment is all.

Everything happens now at the time of the presentation. For example, though I have no data to validate it, I would venture that 89% of all major decisions are made at the time of a presentation and not afterwards. The moment is all-important and – assuming no major decision-makers are absent – the nature of the brain is that many conscious and unconscious processes will be in place and making decisions "live". Hence, the role of what comes after the live presentation is going to be far less important than is often assumed: more of a rubber-stamp, a papal imprimatur ("let it be printed") or some follow-up information to verify a question that was raised at the time.

As business people have become ever-busier, less time is spent going back to presentation decks, and the window between seeing a presentation and making key decisions has shrunk analogously to "theatrical release to DVD" in the cinema world. The opportunity to affect decisions is almost certainly going to happen at the moment of the face-to-face presentation.

Finally, on a personal level, the presentation is the chance for the presenter (let's call them "you") to shine and make, or manage, an impression.

DECK 2

On the other hand, Deck 2, the "leave behind", is an altogether different beast.

Its primary role is not to communicate the findings and insights (this will almost certainly have occurred at the original meeting) but to act as a reference to which those who were there can return (though my experience is that happens far less than is commonly thought, even in competitive agency pitches). It also acts as a second-hand "book of the film" for those who didn't make it to Geneva.

For some, it will therefore offer the chance to delve beneath the surface and check their memory against the written record as a glorified contact report; or give them a chance to delve beneath the surface into the details.

In some ways there are parallels between Deck 1 and Deck 2 and the System 1 and System 2 cognitive systems. Deck 1 should feel more natural, intuitive and spontaneous. Deck 2, on the other hand, should be the more rational, calculating and measured response.

But I remain convinced that the importance of the "leave behind" has deteriorated as the demands of the moment have become paramount. It is a pale imitation of the presentation in influence.

And yet......

and yet, we still lazily make the assumption that one deck will be good enough for both tasks.

My two-tier tips are as follows:
1. Start with a hypothesis (or several) and see which can become the central skeleton for the presentation, the golden thread that will lead you, and your audience, through what you have found and want to communicate.
2. Prepare what I call the VLE (the very long edit), which actor and comedian Will Ferrell labelled his "vomit draft". Sweat out all the information, think more and prepare the alternative angles you can take. Allow your mind to incubate and avoid the confirmation bias of only seeking out material to verify what you want to verify [or worse still, what you think your audience want verified].
3. When you have a comprehensive VLE which still has a golden thread of which you are proud, spend time on both a title that does it justice [see Tip 23] and an introduction that will attract attention and encourage involvement from the start [see Tip 7].
4. Seek advice from colleagues, or even expose some of this to your main contact or the person/people you will be aiming to influence shortly.
5. This then is your "leave behind".
6. Now – and this is very important: leave that behind.
7. Start afresh and work on it as if this deck is not yours and has fallen into your hands by some mysterious Coen brothers' deceit.

Your task is now to render it "fit to present". This is not as easy as you think.

8. First, edit, reduce and simplify. "Write less and think more", as we said before. Always recall that summaries can be as effective as full chapters and that you can always have back up ready (hidden charts, other physical material or even something you can rehearse in your head).

9. Make sure the signposting is clear, simple and expressed in dramatic terms, rather than tired marketing-speak.

10. Ensure the material is presented in a manner that appeals to the emotions of those present, and is also communicated in a way that feels like it addresses their most significant business issues, rather than "some stuff I have done that I'd quite like to say out loud".

11. Reduce it again. Simplify more. Make the language more striking and harpoon-like. Produce something unusual that will live on past its first performance.

12. Make sure the golden thread, the headline and the peak end effects are in place. If so, you will be ready for the final stage. Namely, if you found yourself in a screenplay adapted from a Philip K Dick novel, your laptop was snatched by replicants and the CIA had erased all reference to the material, could you deliver it without any visible means of support?

13. Could you give a five-minute story of the whole presentation that could be taken back to Geneva, assuming the clients hadn't been replaced by androids? If you were a member of the Athenian democracy in 5th century Periclean Athens, you would be expected to have sufficient rhetorical skill to declaim and persuade the assembly of your view. If not, there were plenty of sophists around to take your money in return for helping you "how to make the weak argument the

stronger" as their critics would sneer. As they were particularly well-represented in Athens, a part of the region of Greece known as Attica, this gave rise to the expression "cash in the attic."

PRESENTATION VS. LEAVE BEHIND

Communicate findings
Persuasion
Drama and Theatre
Engage AUDIENCE
All happens NOW
Sell yourself

Reference
Go back and delve
Details
Non-important people

TIP 20: AVOIDING THE LINEAR

Always try to escape the natural tendency to say, do or present something that is little more than a series of "and then... and then..."

I have lost count of the number of presentations I have attended that have been Sellotaped sections from different writers, or merely an assemblage of one-chart-after-another, presented without any golden thread, or linking thought or attempt to help the audience determine where they are or where they are going.

The biographer Michael Holroyd puts it neatly:

"When you write biography or history or non-fiction you always look for a way of escaping from the prison of chronology before you come back into it ......"

It is perfectly possible to escape the confines of linear narrative.

Movies such as *Memento* (narrated backwards), *Groundhog Day* (which we encountered earlier on, or perhaps not) and *Source Code*; novels like David Mitchell's *Cloud Atlas* and TV series such as *Lost* or *Doctor Who* all play games with linear narrative, moving backwards and forwards, interweaving different stories, narrators, timeframes and points of view. These owe much to writers such as Italo Calvino, author of *If On A Winter's Night a Traveller*, a deeply imaginative novel where each chapter breaks off before the next one commences in a different vein. Argentine writer Jorge Luis Borges was also a creator of such labyrinthine puzzles.

This is no doubt a reflection of cultural changes in storytelling, driven in part by the emergence of new forms of non-linear narrative chiefly from the world of gaming. This new language from *Sim City*, *Grand Theft Auto* or *LA Noire* is more complex, iterative and immersive, characterized by cascades and fractals, stories that nest within stories, and has been absorbed by the Hollywood and TV mainstream. *Game of Thrones*, anyone?

And this is without mentioning fan fiction, which has seen the user-generated content model enter the domain of fiction, creating new riffs and mixes of the likes of *Star Trek*, *Harry Potter*, and *Fifty Shades of Grey*.

So be experimental: there is another way of presenting which is not just chronological but can take people on a journey that – providing the golden thread is tight enough – will keep them intrigued and immersed.

TIP 21: **SURPRISE AND MYSTERY**

Surprisingly, surprise is something that is given relatively little attention in the construction of business communication.

Surprise is one of the "big six" universal human emotions and so is something that we all appreciate in a good story as in life, as well as being part of serendipity.

Cinematically, just think of the "oh, so he's dead all along", "she's actually a man" or "he's actually his mother". In the lexicon of horror movies, there is a term for moment of heightened shock: "chair-jumper" shots.

In what is described as the contrast effect, you should use surprise sparingly: no-one likes too many surprises, and the pattern which the surprise is intended to disrupt then becomes too chaotic. The bizarre, it appears, is best remembered when located in the context of a normal storyline and when it suddenly departs from the expected. For maximum benefit, the research suggests that events should also violate just one fundamental principle.

So ponder how to use a surprise to galvanize your gathering into action.

This may occur early on in the proceeding, as screenwriters define as the "inciting incident", such as an event that disturbs the status quo. Think of the cyclone that acts as the catalyst at the start of *The Wizard of Oz*, one of the most literal acts of chaos and disorder at the start of any story.

Or you may choose to unveil your surprise later on in the proceedings, after building some tension earlier on. But be careful about surprise, as many recipients of this gift do not welcome it in the way it was intended. Ensure, if you have a surprise up your magician's sleeve, that you have either cleared it with one of your attendees or have a good sense of what they will accept as surprise.

Biologically, we seem prone to tension and suspense. There are certain nerve cells which respond to uncertainty. What has been called the "pleasure of maybe" indicates that uncertainty is in itself rewarding.

In one experiment involving the scanning of subjects making investment decisions, different parts of the brain lit up according to whether the risky or safe option was selected. The riskier option was associated with the nucleus accumbens, a region linked to pleasure and desire. When the safe option was being considered, however, an area linked with pain and displeasure lit up.

LOST IN MYSTERY

Cousin to surprise and tension in the emotional family is mystery. Someone who has demonstrated mastery of mystery is writer/director JJ Abrams, creator of *Lost*, *Alias* and *Alcatraz* for TV, as well as *Cloverfield*, *Star Trek*, the new *Star Wars* film, and *Missions of Incremental Degrees of Impossibility*.

At a TED event, Abrams told a wonderful story about his grandfather, and a box he bought as a kid for $15 at magic shop in New York, containing unidentified magic tricks and decorated with a big "?" on the outside. Decades after the young Abrams bought it, the box remains unopened. Why? Because sometimes, he declared, mystery is more important than knowledge and because – with a nod to the mythical Pandora's Box, perhaps – for him it represents hope and infinite potential.

Now the box itself is no great shakes but the story behind it and the metaphor are striking and inspiring. For Abrams *every* story is a mystery box.

What Abrams was saying about mystery was that we are all in thrall to curiosity, gripped by anticipation and the need to decode and find patterns and answers in the world around us: what was in the hatch in *Lost* and what did the numbers mean? What was being transported in the train carriage (box?) that crashes at the start of *Super 8*?

The resolution of the mystery can either be immensely satisfying (the feeling at the end of a really good magic trick), or something of a damp squib. Not every *Lost* fan was impressed with the final revelation.

The mystery box theme has also appeared in everything from *Doctor Who* (what else is the Tardis if not a mystery box?), to the film *"Guardians of the Galaxy"* (where the hero opens up a box from his late mother at the end of the movie), to the finale of *Desperate Housewives*.

So with mystery in mind, consider:

- Should I create my own "mystery box"? Should I withhold information, hold back the "answer" and tease my spectators until the big reveal?
- Is there an answer your audience is waiting for (the magic number that says launch or not launch, air the ad or not)? If the answer is softer, more argumentative, it can still be the centre of "the big reveal".
- What is the basis for it? Can I make mystery my golden thread?

TIP 22: **STORYBOARD YOUR STORY**

Next, a technique that creative people will recognize immediately.

Storyboarding is said to go back to Walt Disney in the 1930s, and is the exercise of imagining or pre-visualizing a movie as a series of (let's call them) cartoon frames, accompanied by space for dialogue or notes.

Storyboards are of great help in hypothesizing and establishing continuity, camera angles, effects and character, plus "point of view" (pov). They allow you to see the structure of your film (or presentation) and express and edit as you go along.

Their use spread, soon after, to the advertising industry as a way of demonstrating how an ad would look (what was in the creative's head that needed to be translated for non-creative clients) at a trifle of the finished cost. It also led to the development of animatics and other derivative material used to test adverts before they air.

I recommend storyboarding your presentation. It is a very useful tool for organizing your thought around the principles we have been discussing here: the golden thread, grabbing them early and the peak end effect.

1. Use Post-Its (or any other form of repositionable stationery with a re-adherable strip of adhesive on the back).

2. Write on each the point you are making. That should not be confused with the data you are showing, or the graphs, or the quote from Einstein, Oscar Wilde or Steve Jobs.

3. Start with the headline (or title) and the golden thread. Work through the golden thread and think about timing and editing. The industry estimate is one minute per chart/slide. Remember that you will inevitably stretch out what you say on the day because spontaneous live verbosity is a universal human truth.

4. Each chart makes a point. Do not feel the need to pad it out, but start by making sure that the flow of the argument (the meaning, the thread) is visible throughout.

5. Later on, you can add data or other elaboration. But the most important role of the storyboard is to prioritize the thread.

6. Yes, this will save time. You may feel that your time is precious and dissipated enough without adding another burden, and when I run storytelling sessions the most common comment is often: "But I don't have the time". (*In fact I usually prepare for the day by writing up the word "time" on a pad, and revealing it as soon as someone finally mentions it live, usually about one hour into the session.*)

7. There are many reasons why it saves time.

   a. First, it makes your end product more effective: more cogent, more persuasive and magnificent

   b. Second, once you have established the habit of storyboarding, finding the golden thread and headlining it will become second nature to your pattern-tate brain

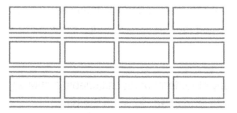

TIP 23: IN LACK OF INTRIGUING HEADLINE SHOCK

So we have started with constructing a golden thread, an argument, a skeleton for the presentation to give us a sense of the whole and have attempted to "start to startle".

The next stage is to find a headline, a title that will create the sense of anticipation and promise.

One of the founding principles of journalism, and what links the most erudite journalism with the new-kid-on-the-block that is Twitter is the significance of a good headline. In the light of everything we saw earlier about priming and patterns and how they set up the brain for what is to come, this should come as no surprise.

Throughout my years of enduring presentations and pitches, it has constantly staggered me that so few of them had an enticing headline that in itself offered a come-hither to the reader/viewer/audience.

GREAT HEADLINES OF OUR TIMES

The former editor of the UK newspaper the Sunday Times (now Sir) Harold Evans once said good headlines should be self-contained telegrams.

"Simplicity, informality and impact are the essence . . . It must be a clear signal; swiftly readable; economical in editorial, production, and reading time, and in newsprint space; proportionate to the news; and flexible."

How many headlines can we recall that have lodged in our memories, compared to the libraries that we have devoured over our lives?

Here is a brief selection of how economy of expression can be so effective:

1. US readers will recognize **"Ford to City: Drop Dead"** from the *New York Daily News* in 1975, in their report of how the president, Gerald Ford, claimed he would veto any bill calling for a federal bail-out of New York City to save it from bankruptcy. In the greatest traditions of journalism, this was evidently not a direct quote from Ford, but it certainly captured the emotional tenor of his approach. It stung, and soon after he changed his stance.

2. US film fans will also recall the headline in *Variety* magazine of 17 July 1935. To capture the sense that rural film-goers of the time were reluctant to see films about their lives which portrayed them as unsophisticated, the front page screamed: **"Sticks Nix Hick Pix"**.

3. No-one who lived through Argentina's invasion of the Falkland Islands (which sparked a ten-week war between Argentina and the UK over the British territories in the South Atlantic) can fail to remember the headline of 4 May, 1982 devised by the tabloid newspaper The Sun after the sinking of the Argentinian ship, the General Belgrano. **"GOTCHA!"** it screamed, in arrogant triumphalism, before the scale of casualties was appreciated.

4. The British, as I'm sure any reader of sophistication will appreciate, are known for a humour based on irony and understatement. So it is not surprising that even in public demonstrations we can have a sense of reserve. During the London demonstrations in 2011, a placard was spotted with the words: "**I'm really not happy about this**". Lovely. It was possibly a subtle reference (students being inherently post-modern and referential) to a famous demonstration, in cult sit-com *Father Ted*, during which Father Ted Crilly and Father Dougal Maguire carried signs saying "**Down With This Sort of Thing**" to protest against the showing of an erotic film called *The Passion of St Tibulus*.

HEADLINING YOURSELF

So how do we learn from some of the great headline acts?

1. In the "attention economy", headlines must be compact and impactful. Look at how many bestselling novels and TV programmes now rely either on the one-worder, or on more exotic and extravagant expressions.
2. This is often counterintuitive to the arithmocracy, which prefers more elaborate, descriptive and dull titles such as *A Research Report into The Behaviour and Attitudes of Industrial Purchasers of Wireless Multi-Function Laser Printers.*
3. They should convey the spirit of the whole piece, be it presentations, research report or sales pitch.
4. This means that as part of the overall process of editing and structure and devising the golden thread, you must define the key idea you are trying to convey. This summarizing and encapsulation is not always automatic, and when I run training sessions I emphasise that the process can often be facilitated collaboratively.

5. This can be any or all of:
   * The main insight (the surprise, the meaning, something the audience is not expecting)
   * The spirit and tone of the piece: this will vary if your audience, or the subjects of your data, are cruise travellers, doctors or video gamers and you should consider this carefully
6. Cheese quotient: by now, you will have seen where I stand on issues of punning, humour wit and cheesiness. Yes, I will often pay homage to the fromage but you may need to consider your audience (as well as your fellow presenters), who may have a different degree of cheese tolerance than you or I have.
7. As you progress through your report or presentation, ensure that all the headlines on your charts or materials tend to the expressive, not just the descriptive.
   * How many times have you seen a headline that merely tells you what a chart is saying (either through the data or a magazine of bullet points)?
   * Why not replace "sales increased during advertising" with "causation or correlation?" or "was it the ads that did it?"

It is more likely to engage the audience (and their attention and minds) if you aim to be more hypothetical, more questioning and more provocative.

SOME EXAMPLES
1. A headline I once devised on the subject of how choice of air fresheners depended on mood and personality was "Scents and Sensibility."
2. A debrief where the key insight was that parents were increasingly leaving their teenagers to play on their PS3, Wii, Gamebox and iPhones was called "Left To Their Own Devices".

3. Working for a major cruise line, I was asked to uncover the barriers to cruising. These all happened to be begin with "C" so the presentations was called "Overcoming C-Sickness"
4. A thought leadership project I carried out for Clear Channel on the future of the outdoor environment was known as "Insight Outside".

TIP 24: DIVINING OR DEVISING A DIVERTING DETAIL

As well devising the golden thread and headline, you finally need to look out for one specific feature too.

A moment's thought (and a slightly more leisurely dip into the psychological research) reveals that a really startling and unanticipated detail can often be the thing that resounds the most, long after the telling.

CRUMBS!

Just take cake and biscuits: surely nothing in our working environments could be any more meaningless and trivial?

So where do biscuits fit in the bigger picture? What great insight can we derive from them?

Now, I know from my experience that most companies are lubricated by cake and biscuits. Whenever I consult with a particular company I can be sure the best companies are those where there is never a shortage of biscuits. I also know that many of the company's social events are based around the preparation and consumption of biscuits and cake.

One of my children recently completed a week of work experience at a central London theatre. After a week of watching rehearsals, working front of house, and being a general factotum, I was keen to find out what was his one overriding insight into the world of art and business.

"They eat a lot of cake" was his pontifical verdict. And he's not wrong.

Or consider this wonderfully opportunistic piece of research-based PR from the UK HQ of Holiday Inn. As reported at the time, four out of five businesses, when asked, claimed that the type of biscuits they served could improve the quality and outcome of a meeting. Lawyers were most impressed by good boardroom biccies, the survey added judiciously. Even more notably, biscuits were ranked ahead of technology, artwork and lighting in the meeting room.

Yes: having the right baked goods was prioritized over getting the laptop to talk to the projector, the lighting to dim over the lectern, or the thermostat neither to fry nor freeze attendees.

But I do think there is a serious conclusion from this assessment of trivia.

First, for a hyper-social species like human beings, the making and eating, but most importantly, the shared conviviality of this ritual oils the wheels of social and commercial activity in the way that we have seen that gossip can.

Second, this seems to me more evidence that much of what is called "content" in our industry is only a means to an end, and that end is conversation. There is a lot of talk, with the boom in social media, about "conversational marketing" and brands as conduits to conversation. Again, I think this explains the importance placed on biscuits.

NOT A PATCH ON CURRENT ADS

Now let's look at a famous ad campaign. In 1951, David Ogilvy of Ogilvy & Mather had been approached by Ellerton Jette, president of CF Hathaway, a small, and pretty much unheard-of, shirt company from Waterville, Maine. Offering only a paltry advertising budget, Jette promised, in return, that he would never alter a word of Ogilvy's copy (manna from heaven for the creative) or ever fire the agency (ditto for the CEO).

After much research, Ogilvy chose an idea based around a distinguished man in a white shirt. But his masterstroke was to ask his model, the aristocratic Baron George Wrangell, to wear a black eye patch over his right eye.

"The Man In the Hathaway Shirt" ad was enormously successful, and was much cited, imitated and lauded at the time. Ogilvy's copy and the photography were also striking, but it is commonly agreed that the eye-patch was crucial to the campaign's success.

But how could a simple prop, one that bore no relevance to the product, have such a profound effect (please note all clients and other persuaders intent on "relevant messaging")?

Ogilvy tapped into something bigger than it appeared to be, at first sight. The eye-patch created a sense of metaphor, mystery and mystique: something that invited the reader to ponder the nature of the incident that had led the character to wear something so noticeable. Advertising thinkers would point to exactly this type of execution to highlight the difference between input (what is actually in the ad) and output (how people seek to decode and respond to it).

Even now, this campaign endures; it was recently voted number 22 in the list of top ad campaigns of all time. Not bad for an idea celebrating its 60th birthday.

THERE IS NOTHING LIKE A DANE

Moving to a more contemporary example, let us explore a Danish diverting detail.

The TV series *Forbrydelsen* [translated as *The Killing*, though the Danish word actually means "Crime"] arrived on the low-key BBC channel BBC 4 in January 2011. It told the story of the murder of 19-year-old Nanna Birk Larsen, and Detective Inspector Sarah Lund. Lund was a strong female character, with a complicated back-story and not especially likeable.

Oh, and did I mention that it was subtitled?

For a minority channel it was a breakout success: more viewers than *Mad Men*, an appreciation index of 94%, even fighting off *Boardwalk Empire*, *Mad Men* and *Glee* to win the international award at the 2011 BAFTAs.

By now, if you were a fellow *Killing* devotee, you will realize what I have chosen not to mention up to this point.

The key to the entire viral spread of The Killing, the topic that followed actress Sofie Gråbøl, who played Lund, was her white Faroese jumper.

It became Lund's trademark, if only because it was such an unlikely wardrobe choice for a cop, at least if you're steeped in the US/UK tradition (few of whose TV detectives were women, at least since Cagney and Lacey).

Gråbøl was bemused that the jumper seemed to dominate discussion of the series:

"It was the only reaction I got! And I thought 'Who cares about the ****ing jumper, why don't you ask me what are we going to do with the story or the character?'"

So, it was the jumper that did it.

Remember this when you fall upon a detail that you think might fuel gossip, something that jumps from detail to emotional carrier.

BRAND DETAIL
Finally, here are three examples from the business world of small details that I think say more about their brand than any expensive, sexy ad campaign could.

The first from "my" Phoenix Cinema in north London, where this sign says a lot about its philosophy and attitude to the sanctity of seeing the film in the right environment; one that precludes the purchase and consumption of noisy crisps for the greater good of a quiet, relaxing viewing experience.

Another example is The Hospital, a members' club in central London that is designed specifically to serve the creative community. In the race to be the coolest and trendiest, these clubs can go to quite extreme lengths, but I really loved this notice on the inside of its lift, which exemplified a quirkiness that would appeal to the sophisticated (and probably quite British) sense of humour of the audience it targets.

Thirdly, this notice affixed to toilets on Virgin trains. Rather than a glib and dull message, it is conveyed with exactly the tongue-in-cheek spirit that characterizes the Virgin brand. Other train lines have since copied it, but it doesn't feel quite the same

CONCLUSION

So we will be well advised to think about that unexpectedly diverting detail that our audience may not see coming in terms of its potential to create a story or dominate gossip.

1. Have we got a "jumper" here?
2. What is it that might colonize people's minds?
3. Is it what we think it is?
4. And is it what we want it to be?

SIDES
OLIVES £2
BREAD £1
HUMOUS £2
CRISPS £1.20
(CRISPS ARE TOO LOUD TO TAKE IN TO T
FILM... SORRY)

9 PERSONS 1000KG

OR

1 HORSE
5,050 BANANAS
6,666 HENS EGGS
2,941 PIGEONS
88 HADDOCK
10,526 POUND COINS

Please
don't flush
Nappies, sanitary towels,
paper towels, gum,
old phones, unpaid bills,
junk mail, your ex's sweater,
hopes, dreams or goldfish

down this
toilet

A HAPPY ENDING

"Happy". Mid-14th century: from "lucky". from "hap", "chance, fortune" (as in haphazard); sense of "very glad" first recorded late 14th century. French "bonheur" shares similar meaning.

There has been a sudden and rather unexpected industry in what academics call "hedonics": the study of happiness. Some have even used the term "hedon" as a unit of happiness.

(An example of how to use this in everyday conversation: if my happiness conflicts with yours, we have a hedon collision.)

So how can storytelling contribute to your personal and professional happiness?

THE STORY OF YOUR HAPPINESS
One of the key conclusions is that creativity generates happiness, in that it creates Professor of psychology Mihaly Csikszentmihalyi's "flow", and a sense of control over your surroundings and life. Feeling happy makes you more curious, playful and creative and the arrow works both ways.

So making yourself happy, and making your clients/audiences happy is good for your business and their business.

1. Give yourself permission to speculate. Develop more hypotheses, as this is one of the first steps on the way to being more creative. The more meaningful and satisfying your

activity at work, the more "flow" time you will generate and the happier you will feel.

2. This also means being more synthetic (opposite of reductive, not opposite of authentic).

3. Be an outsider, remain receptive and maintain an external focus. Pursue fruitful error and do all you can to "de-average" yourself. Look for ways of exploring how human beings make and seek meaning.

4. Remember to stay playful and retain a sense of humour and wit in all situations.

5. Build a PUD folder. Insight, I find, comes from discovering and serendipitously applying "Previously Unapplied Detail" when you are lost or stuck in neutral. Try to regularly fill it (avoiding saying "populate") with ideas, hypotheses and "hmm, interesting". One day your unconscious incubation will thank you.

6. Thinking about the future is also key to a happy life.

HOW CAN YOU MAKE YOURSELF HAPPIER?
THE MASTER THREAD

It seems counterintuitive, but we are more fashioned by our tools rather than vice versa. The computer metaphor has led us to see humans as information processors and message-receivers. Yet it is self-evident that far fewer of our problems can be solved through more information. Information is too often, in the wrong hands, the enemy of inspiration: surprise should be more highly valued.

All of us who purport to be in the information business are actually in the spinning business, the spinners of yarns all looking for the right thread.

Storytelling is a more powerful approach because it is truer to our universal nature, as well as easier to implement and more entertaining.

It can reframe thinking and behaviour, and as such, is closely related to the corpus of knowledge known as behavioural economics.

Story can breach the defences of information, particularly when our dominant operating systems are PowerPoint, Word and Excel. If we need to give shape to "in-form" our thoughts and observations, stories are the elemental and convenient way of doing this. We must learn to stop treating most meetings as dictation.

Story also focuses attention, in a world where our atention has more claims upon it than it ever has before, especially in the business environment. Stories can avoid the pitfalls of CPA and task saturation because they naturally focus attention in a way that steaming piles of data cannot.

And it is not as if we are forcing ourselves to something unnatural: it is part of our species' inheritance to tell, absorb and live through story. It is no etymological surprise that we talk of being "gripped by" a good story: story can hold us in its hand, and it can exert a powerful grip on human cognition in so doing.

Human beings – even we hard-nosed business types – are semavores, meaning-seeking missiles who (if we forget our professional roles for a moment) are generally resistant to being "educated and messaged to/at". So, another way of expressing our role as communicators is as being in the construction and delivery businesses. We are either constructing meaning for semavores, or delivering it.

- Story is a universal framework for organizing ideas and translating data and information into meaning
- It is an automatically System 1-friendly and an emotional way of creating empathy, trust and triggering oxytocin to forge more caring connections
- It is inherently playful and entertaining without looking like it is trivializing
- It is the enemy of distraction as it directs attention, enables gossip and enhances status
- It is the opposite of instruction, and neither didactic nor pedagogic. It is inspiring, enthusiastic and fun
- We need to ensure that we are not adding to the population of deck-heads

Story also forces us to think in hypotheses and "what-ifs" in the way that other scientists and other "creative" people do to broaden their horizons.

Be a storyteller not a lister: outside of students of antiseptic surgery, no-one is interested in listers.

Strive to ensure that the room doesn't think "oh-oh: here comes the data-freighter". Too often, the quantity of content disguises the poverty of thought, the absence of form and the paucity of insight. Researchers, particularly, should beware mistaking weighing their deck for reading it.

I hope not to "empower" but at least give you the courage to dump the dross and the data duvet. No-one wants to hear the "thud" of a giant deck hitting the table, or of the audience losing collective consciousness, if not the will to live.

Storytelling is an antidote to arithmocracy that will make you feel more productive, more effective and, yes, even happier.

THE END.

ABOUT THE AUTHOR

Tas is a man of many lanyards: trainer, author, speaker, brand/comms strategist and lecturer.

He is a course director for the Chartered Institute of Marketing, the Market Research Society, the Institute of Internal Communication and the Civil Service College, and principal advisor for CIO Connect in Hong Kong.

He is a global speaker and regularly reviews the papers and contributes on marketing and communications subjects on TalkTV.

Specialist topics include storytelling, behavioural economics, insightment and briefing ,Tas can be found loitering at **@taswellhill** and **https://www.linkedin.com/in/tastasgal/**

ACKNOWLEDGMENTS AND GRATITUDE

Thanks to Martin for sticking with the book.

Supplications have already been offered to the Gods of Spellcheck, aka Mnay Thnaks (sic) and Sic.

To my loyal and faithful friend the Earl of Grey without whom this – and so much of my life – would never have happened.

Multitudinous thanks to Josh, Zach and Sas for having to put up with me constantly using and explaining the etymology of words like "multitudinous" and for their relentless criticism, some of it occasionally constructive.